Methods for th
of Communica

Methods for the Ethnography of Communication is a guide to conducting ethnographic research in classroom and community settings that introduces students to the field of ethnography of communication and takes them through the recursive and nonlinear cycle of ethnographic research. Drawing on the mnemonic that Hymes used to develop the ethnography of SPEAKING, the authors introduce the innovative CULTURES framework to provide a helpful structure for moving through the complex process of collecting and analyzing ethnographic data and address the larger "how-to" questions that students struggle with when undertaking ethnographic research. Exercises and activities help students make the connection between communicative events, acts, and situations and ways of studying them ethnographically. Integrating a primary focus on language in use within an ethnographic framework makes this book an invaluable core text for courses on ethnography of communication and related areas in a variety of disciplines.

Judith Kaplan-Weinger is Professor in the Linguistics Department at Northeastern Illinois University.

Char Ullman is Associate Professor of Sociocultural Foundations of Education and Educational Anthropology at the University of Texas at El Paso.

Methods for the Ethnography of Communication

Language in Use in Schools and Communities

Judith Kaplan-Weinger and Char Ullman
*Northeastern Illinois University and
the University of Texas at El Paso*

Routledge
Taylor & Francis Group

NEW YORK AND LONDON

First published 2015
by Routledge
711 Third Avenue, New York, NY 10017

and by Routledge
2 Park Square, Milton Park, Abingdon, Oxon, OX14 4RN

Routledge is an imprint of the Taylor & Francis Group, an informa business

Library of Congress Cataloging-in-Publication Data
Kaplan-Weinger, Judith, author.
  Methods for the ethnography of communication : language in use in schools and communities / Judith Kaplan-Weinger and Char Ullman ; Northeastern Illinois University and the University of Texas El Paso.
    p. cm
  1. Intercultural communication—Study and teaching.   2. Intercultural communication–Social aspects.   3. Language and culture—Study and teaching.
4. Language and culture—Social aspects.   5. Ethnology—Research—Social aspects.
6. Educational equalization—Social aspects.   7. Anthropological linguistics.
I. Ullman, Char, author.   II. Title.
  P53.255.K36 2015
  418.0071—dc23
  2014024367

ISBN: 978-0-415-51776-8 (hbk)
ISBN: 978-0-415-51777-5 (pbk)
ISBN: 978-0-203-12376-8 (ebk)

Typeset in Utopia
by Apex CoVantage, LLC

Contents ●●●●●

Preface ●●●●●

As students, there are courses we step into—sometimes with excited anticipation for what we will learn, other times with trepidation for what we will have to do—that change our lives. The content may be so new to us, or the activities assigned may be so enjoyably challenging, or the perspective may be so meaningful that our lives grow beyond the boundaries of an academic subject to encompass a new way of thinking, even a new way of life. Such is the effect on us of the courses we have taken in the ethnography of communication. We learned through those courses that the ethnography of communication is more than a subject, course title, or textbook. It is a perspective that influences the learner to adopt new knowledge, new understanding, and new appreciation for the values and behaviors that unite as well as distinguish human communities.

By opening this textbook, you have initiated a life change. Your experiences as you traverse the chapters that follow will take you, as Michael Agar (1994) explains, from "[a] life of Being . . . into a life of Becoming" (p. 28). Whoever you now are—

- a linguistics major;
- a communication studies major;
- an anthropology major;
- a business major;
- an education major;
- a nursing/public health major;
- a student being introduced to a new academic field;
- a graduate student honing your skills in research and analysis;
- a teacher in the midst of choosing a textbook that increases your knowledge and skills as it helps to educate your students; or
- a professional tasked with researching a community of teachers and learners, corporate workers, or medical personnel;

—*Methods for the Ethnography of Communication: Language in Use in Schools and Communities* will engage you in the fieldwork and analysis of naturally occurring actions and interactions. Along the way, you will also acquire a strong theoretical foundation in which to situate your research; competence in applying a model that guides the observation, interviewing, and artifact analysis central to your research; and an understanding of the reasons for and effects of sharing your research with a variety of stakeholders.

Methods for the Ethnography of Communication contains exercises and activities that demonstrate the connection between communicative events, acts, and situations and ways of studying them ethnographically. As you complete the exercises and activities that prepare you for and take you through ethnographic data collection and analysis, you will read excerpts of foundational essays in the fields of anthropology, linguistics, and education that use the techniques you have practiced. We introduce the field of ethnography of communication through primary sources including landmark essays in the field of ethnographic theory and application, samples of ethnographic research done by scholars and students, and discussions of the role of ethnographic research in a variety of settings (academic, corporate, political, geographic, religious, recreational, and community based). Additionally, this text addresses the cognitive component of social interaction through examining the influence of language use on cognition and culture. Finally, this text teaches the 'how-to's' of ethnographic data collection and analysis as it takes students through a cyclical research framework encompassing the process of planning data collection (including initiating community engagement and completing and submitting an Internal Review Board (IRB) proposal), gathering data, analyzing data, and presenting findings. At every stage of the process, in- and out-of-class activities are offered so students can practice applying the framework in the search for patterns in natural behavior, the identification of the ideologies that motivate those patterns, and the recognition of the identities constructed and presented through those patterns.

Central to this text are two innovative contributions to the ethnography of communication. The first is a process framework that accompanies students through an ethnographic research project in the space of a quarter- or semester-long course. The second is a discussion of social theory and its implications for and applications to ethnographic inquiry. Foundational concepts and researchers are discussed throughout the text as students gain a strong grounding in undertaking fieldwork and analysis in the context of theories of social interaction. You will consider how ethnographic knowledge is produced and explore issues of epistemology. You will be guided to call up your background knowledge about a community of practice you wish to study, and about other communities that are similar to or different from it. You will also consider knowledge production and your own positionality as you come to recognize that your histories, experiences, and expectations influence your perceptions and, therefore, what you see and understand to be meaningful in other communities.

In the context of social theory, the ethnography of communication is presented and undertaken as an epistemological endeavor for both community participants and researchers. Because cultural meaning is constructed and re-constructed continually, any given community has the potential to be understood in a vast number of ways. The goal of our text is to lead you through a process of knowing—to help you consider what you bring to your analysis of interactions and to help you develop the tools for gathering and analyzing data in a way that both affirms that knowledge and preserves what is meaningful to those you study. We promise that this course will transform you both intellectually and personally. You will come to see the world and those who interact within it in new ways. And you will leave with skills that you will forever be able to apply as your desire to 'become' and not just 'be' ever increases.

Reference

Agar, M. (1994). *Language shock: Understanding the culture of conversation.* New York: HarperCollins.

Acknowledgments ● ● ● ● ●

With gratitude, we acknowledge the contributions of the following people who shared their data with us, as well as their insights and their expertise:

Dr. Katherine Mortimer, University of Texas at El Paso; Dr. Christina Convertino, University of Texas at El Paso; Amira Sebai, Northeastern Illinois University; Ahlam Almohissen, Northeastern Illinois University; and Rawan Bonais, Northeastern Illinois University.

And a special cheer goes out to Jair Muñoz, doctoral student at the University of Texas at El Paso, editorial work and creating an index for the book. We also thank our editors at Routledge, who believed in this project from the start.

1

• • • • •

Making the Familiar Strange, Making the Strange Familiar

"Welcome to this class." These are words your professor may have uttered or will utter on your first day in the class that is using this text. Settling into a new classroom is a common experience, open to causing enthusiasm or angst, wonder or dread, boredom or indifference. And your feelings may not be one or the other (i.e., binaries) but a complicated mixture of these emotions.

Thinking Together

As you entered the classroom, you were met with images and sounds that were probably familiar to you.

1. What are some of those images? Sounds?
2. Why are they familiar to you?

It is also possible that you were met with images and sounds that were unfamiliar to you.

3. What are some of those images? Sounds?
4. Why are they unfamiliar to you?

While you may be thinking of classrooms where you have been a student in the past, we are asking you, first, to explain what you see and hear in this classroom. Then, you will analyze those sensory experiences in relation to your own personal history.

Faced with this collection of the known and unknown, you likely felt at least a bit unsettled. That feeling, of course, may have been below your consciousness. Maybe you felt it only in the decision you needed to make about what desk or chair to sit in, or what to say, if anything, to the people sitting near you. It may also have been about what language or what style of language to use to address the people around you.

Thinking Together

1. Are you someone who talks to people you don't know?
2. Do you initiate conversations, or do you wait until someone talks to you?
3. If you do initiate conversations, how do you do that?

There will be classmates who introduce themselves to each other, and those who don't. There will be those who talk and participate, and those who do not. There may be people who are reading this text in English and speaking with you in English, but who use other languages most of the time.

In the United States, we often chalk this up to individual differences, by focusing on personality traits such as confidence/shyness or extroversion/introversion. Indeed, our particular traits impact how we act in different situations. However, there are multiple factors that influence our behavior.

● ● ● ● ●

Globalized Worlds

We live in a globalized world today. That means that people and nations are more connected than ever before, whether it is through transportation, technology, or both. Most people make use of a variety of cultural systems in their everyday lives. It is this idea of **cultures** that we will explore throughout this text.

The concept of culture has been central to the fields of anthropology, linguistics, education, and communication studies, but none of these disciplines has ownership of the idea of culture. Business people talk about marketing to different cultural groups; physicians discuss cultural competence in delivering health care; educators practice culturally relevant pedagogy; and the list goes on and on. If you still go to a physical library, the GN section (using the Library of Congress system) is filled with book after book that grapples with what culture is and even whether it even exists at all. If you Google the word *culture* you will be looking at links for days (including information on how to make yogurt). Even though culture is a fundamental concept in the social sciences and in education, there is no longer clear agreement on just what it is.

Up until 1980 or so, scholars thought about culture as a structure that existed outside of the individual, that firmly governed human behavior, and that never changed. There has been a revolution in how people think about culture since then. Now, it is more likely for people to think about culture(s) in the plural and to think about them as processual.

Gonzalez, Moll, and Amanti (2005) encourage us to see culture as the practices we engage in every day. Culture is "what it is that people do and what they say about what they do" (p. 40).

Henze and Hauser (1999) note seven characteristics of the contemporary concept of culture:

1. **Culture is not bounded for most people who live in urban areas.** While there are Indigenous people whose communities are composed of people almost exclusively from the same background and who live in remote areas, most people in urban areas throughout the world live in relationship to people from different backgrounds. Culture is more fluid than bounded.

2. **Cultural groups vary a lot.** There are many ways to be a member of a group. There is more than one way to be Mexican or to be Jewish or to be gay, or to be Jewish, Mexican, and gay. No one person holds all the knowledge for her group. The things we know depend on many things, such as our age, gender, class, sexuality, religion, ability, and many other aspects of identity. Our histories are also a part of what it means to be a member of a cultural group.

3. **Cultures are constantly changing.** We construct our cultural knowledge and practices all the time, so they are not static. Your grandmother and grandfather may share your cultural background, but you might have very different ways of being a woman or a man, or of engaging in your cultural practices, than they do. Think about the way many people in their 60s talk and dress. It is often very different from people in their 20s.

4. **Cultural knowledge is often below our consciousness.** Many times we do what we do and think what we think because that is how we were socialized in our families and our communities. That is, people modeled behaviors for us, and we were either rewarded for learning to do things "correctly" or punished for doing things "wrong". Eventually, we learned to become members of different cultural groups, and those behaviors and beliefs got to be second nature.

5. **Cultural knowledge impacts how we interpret the world around us.** Some theorists think that having common ways of understanding or interpreting the world around us is the most important part

of culture. Consider this: An 11-month-old toddler takes a toy truck away from her five-year-old brother and hits him with it. Her brother is injured and starts to bleed. In European-American cultures, it is common to take the toy away from the toddler and get the toddler to understand that she has hurt her brother. There is a belief that the rules of the adult world apply equally to this newcomer to the planet. In Mayan cultures, it is common to let the toddler do what she does. One-year-old newcomers are not expected to follow adult rules, because there is a belief that toddlers cannot do things on purpose or understand that they have hurt someone else yet (Mosier and Rogoff, 2003). These are examples of shared cultural interpretations.

6. **Culture is in our everyday practices.** If you think about the previous scene with the toddler, culture is in the ways people behave. Do you take the toy away, or do you let the toddler play with it? Culture is in our lived experiences, our cultural practices. This is an example of the idea that culture is processual (Gonzalez, 2008), and not *just* in that shared interpretation.

7. **Culture(s) give us certain positions and biases.** All of us experience the world through our memberships in cultural groups. If you were raised by human beings, then you learned to be a member of at least one cultural group. If you were not raised by human beings, well, you probably aren't reading this book. Think about what the world looks like through the lens of a camera. What you can see depends on where you are standing.

Your teacher may have started today's class with an activity to help you and your classmates get to know one another. In the field of education, these activities are called icebreakers.

Thinking Together

1. What is the ice that needs to be broken in a classroom?
2. Why do teachers want to break that ice?
3. Why is it important that students break that ice?

Just like authentic ice, the ice that exists among members of a community can be hard and slippery to navigate. We can stumble or fall on the ice, and we can even slip through the ice. But we can also glide. This metaphor helps us realize that joining a new community can be challenging for everyone. Yet, at the same time, breaking the ice—the coldness that causes us to feel separate from one another—can help remove much of the challenge so that we—students together, and instructor and students together—can collectively create an environment that best eases teaching and learning and, therefore, best lays down the tracks for us all to reach our educational goals.

Building community is important in most situations. Sometimes communities form on their own. That is typically what occurs in a classroom community. None of us is new to a classroom environment, although we may never have shared the very same classroom with anyone who is now in our class. And we may have been in classrooms in the past that are very different from this one. In many classrooms, students raise their hands to get the teacher to call on them, right? In the Mexican state of Sonora, students do that too, but in many public schools there, it is still the tradition to stand when you give your answer to the class. Regardless of the kind of school settings that are part of our personal histories, we bring what we know from those earlier classrooms with us into this classroom. If we have shared a prior class with a current classmate, some of what we know and some of what we expect to occur in this class will be based on that prior experience, too.

Learning to Look

1. What do you expect of this classroom?
2. What is here?
3. How will it be used?
4. Who is here?
5. What will they do?
6. How will you interact with them?

● ● ● ● ●

Building Schema

What you have just talked about is reflective of the kind of knowledge you bring with you to every place you go and everything you do. Your mind is full of expectations based on the prior experiences you have. This knowledge is your **schema**—the background knowledge you have that leads you to construct a framework for seeing, organizing, and making sense of what is in your world. You most often call upon your schema without thought. In other words, your schema kicks in or is activated when you enter into a situation that you have had some previous experience with. There is no specific amount of experience—no time length, no number of interactions—you need in order for your knowledge to accumulate and your schema to be ready to guide you through new experiences.

For example, Char is from the United States but has lived in Mexico and in Ecuador. While there are markets where people barter in the United States, she had never been to one until she went to Merida, Yucatán, Mexico. Buying fruits and vegetables at an open-air Mexican market is different from buying them at a grocery store in the United States, where the prices are set. Here are some of the schema she developed to shop at a Mexican market:

- Have a general idea of what things cost.
- Bring your own bags.
- If you want bargains, go to the market right before it closes for the day. You may not find something specific you are looking for, but often the vendors will give you something extra, because they do not want to carry a lot of produce home.
- Bring cash.
- Make sure you have small bills. If you bargain for something and say you have only a certain amount of money, you are exposed as a liar if you present a large bill. Also, the vendor may not have change.
- If you want to get a good deal, organize your cash so that the small bills are visible and the large bills are not.
- If you see something you were looking for and it is ripe, do not out-wardly express excitement about it. Vendors will charge you more if they think you really want it.
- The first price that the vendor gives is often inflated, because you are expected to bargain.
- Bargain. Going to the market is not just a way to buy food but also a way of being social.
- You can ask to taste something.
- If you do not think the produce is fresh, or if you think the price is too high, it is OK to say so and walk to the next stall. Sometimes the vendor will run after you and give you a better price.
- You cannot return anything.

Char did not learn these things after her first visit to the market. It took five or six visits and conversations with Mexican friends.

Thinking Together

1. Is the schema she described one that you share?
2. What is your schema for buying fruits and vegetables?

The greater your prior knowledge, the more accurate your expectations are likely to be, and the more comfortable this new experience will end up being. It may be so comfortable, in fact, that you take no notice of it at all. Everything and everyone in the classroom may feel 'just right' to you, allowing you to move on to focusing on what you are there to learn. On the contrary, some things and some people may seem unusual to you, violate your expectations, and even, possibly, disrupt your learning. How possible is it, though, that everything and everyone will be new to you? Probably not too possible. Even if much is new and unexpected, your schema will quickly allow you to compensate and provide you with enough background to get through at least the first day. As you do, your mind will be aching for more information and devouring all that comes its way. All that is new will be quite noticeable to you and, unless you turn away, will settle in with your previous experiences to further expand your schema and, in turn, provide that needed foundation for understanding your community. The sociologist C. Wright Mills was famous for saying, although some credit the poet Friedrich von Hardenberg (pen name Novalis) as the originator, that the social scientist's job was to "make the strange familiar and make the familiar strange". That is, he wanted researchers to question their assumptions about things that they saw and heard every day, in the same way that they questioned things that they had not seen and heard every day.

●●●●●

Communities

We've so far used the classroom as our example community. There are many more communities you are a member of as well. Think about some of your other communities. At one time, you were a new member, and since that first day of membership, you have continued to build knowledge of and comfort within that group.

For example, Judy grew up in a secular Jewish family, and she, her husband, and their four children now practice what is called Traditional Judaism. They keep kosher, which means they eat foods that follow certain standards identified in religious texts, and they observe the weekly Sabbath by attending synagogue services, not driving, and refraining from work. Judy's children attended religious day schools where half of their day was devoted to studying the Hebrew language, Jewish history, and religious texts, and the other half was spent on math, history, science, and English composition and literature classes. All of her children play musical instruments, and while in school they played softball or baseball, worked on their schools' yearbooks, and volunteered at various charitable organizations. Life for Judy and her family, like for many of us, straddles a variety of communities, each with some unique expectations of what its members will believe, do, and say.

Char was raised to be heterosexual, as most people are. That is, today some people's parents want their children to embrace whatever sexual orientation they have. That wasn't how it was for Char back in the 1960s. Her mother had caught her kissing another girl at age nine. In 10th grade, her mother pulled the heart necklace that another girl had given her off her neck. In her family, it wasn't "cool" to be queer, so she hid it for a while. She began coming out as a lesbian to herself, her family, and her friends when she was 21, way back in 1983. The first time Char went to a lesbian bar with the intention of meeting women was at a place called the Lady Bug, on the north side of Chicago. At that time, the bars were racially segregated (not by law but by practice), and she was a White woman in a White bar. She walked up to the bar to order a beer, and it was clear that she was an outsider. Why? She didn't walk right, she didn't dress right, she smiled too much, and she was wearing nail polish. And her earrings were too big. These were the days of Lesbian Separatism (i.e., a philosophy that was about women living separately from men). It was a very political time. People would say, "Feminism is the theory; Lesbianism is the practice." Gay men and lesbians had a lot of conflict then (it was before the AIDS/HIV crisis brought the two groups together), and Char didn't know how things worked. But she was a fast study. Two weeks later, she had the right buzzed haircut and the right thrift-store plaid shirts, and she was reading feminist theory and listening to what was then called "women's music" (e.g., Ferron, Chris Williamson, Meg Christian). Soon, she was asking women to dance, and they were even saying "yes". This is an example of entering a community. Twenty years later, she identifies as queer, what she sees as a more inclusive identity than lesbian, which still smacks of the separatist days for her, and she and her partner have a sign at their front door that says, "Homo Home". Oh, and they were among the first same-sex couples to get married in New Mexico in 2013.

There are, of course, regional communities—your hometown, the city you live in now, an area you hang out in, a city where you have worked or where you have family. Not all communities are regional, however. Many people participate in transnational communities. That is, they have identity ties in more than one nation. They may have part of their family and friend network in one country, and part in another. We will think of **communities** for now as groups of people who interact with one another for some reason. That interaction might happen through the internet, through plane travel, or through riding the same bus to work or school every day. For our purposes, a community might be people who work in the same office or who belong to the same organization. They could be the people in your singing group. They could be high school friends that you are still in touch with through Facebook; an online gaming community you participate in; friends and family in Mexico, whom you see each year and talk to online or by phone; or your extended family who live in another part of the United States.

To make this concept more concrete, let's talk about a community that you are an active member of and an experience within that community that is very common to you.

Talking Together

1. What is one community you are an active member of?
2. What are the expectations of how people should act in this community? (E.g., Judy's example is that Orthodox Jewish women are expected to wear modest clothing that covers them from the collarbone to mid-calf.)

Now think about how you know what to do and even what to say when you are in this community. Most likely, this is a question you've never thought about, or, if you have, you thought about it when you first became a member, but you don't anymore. That's because your knowledge of how to interact in the different communities you belong to and of what to expect of others in the community has become tacit or passive knowledge. You simply don't think about it; you just use it and it works. You successfully interact because what you do and who you do it with all feel normal and like second nature to you.

When you participate in your communities as is expected without actively depending on or being aware of your knowledge, you are making use of **tacit knowledge**. In contrast, when you actively call upon that knowledge so you can participate as is expected, you are making use of **explicit knowledge**. Because this knowledge is knowledge about a community and the norms or rules one must follow to be a member, we call it **cultural knowledge**. Tacit knowledge is passive knowledge. It lies below the level of awareness but still quite competently allows one to interact appropriately with others in the community. Here's an example: Char belongs to an LGBTQ and Allies chorus. Some of the people in the chorus read music, and some don't. The people who don't read music listen to their parts on CDs and get some help with reading music at rehearsals. Char reads music, so her musical knowledge is tacit. She doesn't have to think about it. Explicit knowledge is active knowledge. It lies on the level of awareness and must be consciously drawn on so you may interact appropriately within the community. Some of the other altos who don't read music have asked her questions about things like key signatures and rests. In those moments, Char calls on her explicit knowledge to explain things about reading music.

Thinking Together

1. When do you call upon tacit knowledge in your community?
2. What does this knowledge allow you to do or say?
3. Do you remember a time you called upon explicit cultural knowledge?
4. Why did you need to?
5. Did it help you?
6. Did it provide you with all you needed to know to interact appropriately?

●●●●●

What Does It Mean to Be Competent?

All of us are competent in many areas. At the same time, we all have things that we are still learning. Think of five activities you have some competence in, such as making salsa, posting on Facebook, wearing hijab, changing the oil in your car, etc. . . .

Reflecting Together

Work with a partner. Fill in five activities in which you have some degree of competence. Then, rate your level of competence for each activity by circling the 1, 2, 3, 4, or 5.

	Activity	Level of Competence (5 is highest, 1 lowest)				
1.		5	4	3	2	1
2.		5	4	3	2	1
3.		5	4	3	2	1
4.		5	4	3	2	1
5.		5	4	3	2	1

The knowledge you possess that guides you in your interactions—whether they be in the classroom, on the sports field, or at your job—is something you have acquired throughout your lifetime. That knowledge is flexible and can expand and change as you continue to experience the world. For Judy, teaching comes to mind when she considers how her knowledge set has grown and transformed over time. Judy has taught linguistics for over thirty years. When she entered classes in her very early years of teaching, she brought notes with her, and she relied on those notes as she lectured and when she led her students in class discussions. After those first few years, however, Judy found she no longer needed notes. She trusted her knowledge; she believed that her class preparation and her experience in the classroom would get her through each session. Judy continues to prepare for each class, but she has grown comfortable enough to let discussions develop as she teaches. She is freer in her teaching and hopes her students feel more engaged in learning. One concern Judy has is her aging memory; she says quite often that she will know when it's time to retire when she feels she has to return to those notes.

●●●●●

Funds of Knowledge

Our knowledge is not just individual. Families and groups have gathered knowledge throughout history, or they would not have survived until today. We accumulate knowledge that helps us as members of households to function and maintain our well-being. The knowledge and skills that we develop as members of households are called **funds of knowledge** (Greenberg, 1989; Gonzalez, Moll, and Amanti, 2005; Velez-Ibanez and Greenberg, 1992). All of us are competent and have knowledge that comes from our lived experiences.

Knowledge is not just stored in our heads. It's in our communities. It is through our interactions with other members of our communities that we learn to behave in ways that are in keeping with our group. Knowledge stored is knowledge that leads us to interact as expected with members of our communities. Knowledge stored leads us to follow norms of interaction. There is a range of appropriate ways to participate in a cultural scene, and much depends on the positions we hold.

When we act appropriately, we follow the norms. However, when people act inappropriately, either because they disagree with certain norms or because they do not possess the knowledge necessary to guide them, others may question their participation in the activity or even their membership in the community. **Not all norms are created equally.** That is, some norms of interaction are more important than others. For example, on the U.S.-Mexico border, it's common for people to kiss each other on the cheek when they say hello and when they say goodbye. This is also common throughout Latin America. The person who fails to do this is considered *mal educad@* (the @ is used here to include both the masculine and feminine form of the word, because the @ sign includes an -a and an -o in it), which means "impolite" or "poorly raised". The fact that there is a term to label people who don't follow certain norms means that there are people who, well, don't always follow those norms. That is, if you don't say goodbye to everyone at a party by kissing them on the cheek, you don't lose your status as a member of the community. You're just *mal educad@*. But if you belong to a religious group that does not accept LGBTQ people, for example, and you come out as gay, you are likely to lose your group membership.

●●●●●

Communicative Competence

In sociolinguistics, a field that has close ties to the ethnography of communication, when someone has mastered the norms of interaction that lead to appropriate participation in a community, one has **communicative competence**. Coined by the father of the ethnography of communication, Dell Hymes, in 1966, communicative competence can be defined as knowledge of how to use language appropriately within various communities and various situations.

In Hymes' words, "the study of communicative competence is seen as an aspect of what from another angle may be called the ethnography of symbolic forms—the study of the variety of genres, narration, dance, drama, song, instrumental music, visual art, that interrelate with speech in the communicative life of a society. . . ." (1972, pp. 283–284) It is the interrelationship between speech or language and what members of a community do to show that they know how to participate in that community that is the focus of research within the perspective of the ethnography of communication and its goal of investigating how language is used to both constitute and describe communal identity. Because the concept of communicative competence can be a part of doing the ethnography of communication, let's look at various ways scholars have defined the term:

> Erving Goffman (1982) was a sociologist who researched interaction through a dramaturgical perspective. For him, participants in interaction present a self to others through their actions, including talk. Participants strive through their use of language and other actions to be accepted in the role they present. To be communicatively competent, then, participants must use language appropriately so their audience accepts the role they have chosen to adopt.

> Michael Canale and Merrill Swain (1980) and Canale (1983) adapted Hymes' concept of communicative competence to language teaching and learning. They initially constructed a three-part model of communicative competence that includes (1) grammatical competence—knowledge of the linguistic components

of language including sounds, words and parts of words, sentence structures, and meanings; (2) sociolinguistic competence—knowledge of how to use these components appropriately in natural interactions; and (3) strategic competence—possession of a set of techniques for communicating, including asking questions when in need of information, using directives when you want others to undertake tasks, and, when you forget a word, choosing to describe what you mean rather than name it. Canale (1983) later added discourse competence—the knowledge of how to use language to maintain coherence and cohesion in talk—to this model of communicative competence.

James Paul Gee (1996) described communicative competence as something that we cannot learn from a book. It's something that, for him, comes only from being apprenticed to a member of the community. Participating appropriately within a community means knowing the discourse of that community. For Gee, a discourse is a kind of 'identity kit' that comes complete with an "appropriate costume and instructions on how to act, talk, and often write, so as to take on a particular role that others will recognize" (p. 127). He calls the communicative competence of our homes our *primary discourse*. He calls other discourses that we have to learn and be apprenticed to *secondary discourses*. The discourse of schools and education is a secondary discourse for many of us.

Lyle Bachman (1990) offered a model of language competence that, although differing in title, is similar to Canale and Swain's model. Bachman sees language competence as composed of organizational competence (roughly, Canale and Swain's grammatical and discourse competencies) and pragmatic competence, which focuses, first, on the functions one performs with language and, second, on appropriate language choices one makes from among a variety of possibilities in accordance with existent situational and cultural expectations and constraints.

Thinking Together

1. What do you think about the idea of communicative competence?

2. A good way to ensure that you understand new concepts is to be able to paraphrase them. With reference, then, to communicative competence, let's create our own class definition that we can use as we continue to explore language in use.

●●●●●
Wrapping Up

We're starting to think about the idea of culture and the various groups to which we belong. We're also starting to think about how the ways we use language are key to how we participate in different groups. In the next chapter, we will delve more deeply into the foundation of the ethnography of communication—a foundation that is constructed out of the common concerns of the fields of linguistics and anthropology.

This article and others that appear in various chapters as examples of ethnographic inquiry can be accessed through your university library, and the information you need to search for them is available in the References section at the end of this chapter:

●●●●●
References

Bachman, L. F. (1990). *Fundamental considerations in language testing*. Oxford: Oxford University Press.

Canale, M. (1983). From communicative competence to communicative language pedagogy. In Richards, J. C., & Schmidt, R. W. (Eds.), *Language and communication* (pp. 2–27). London: Longman.

Canale, M., & Swain, M. (1980). Theoretical bases of communicative approaches to second language teaching and testing. *Applied Linguistics, 1*, 1–47.

Gee, J. P. (1996). *Social linguistics and literacies* (2nd ed.). London: Taylor and Francis.

Goffman, E. (1982). *Interaction ritual: Essays on face-to-face behavior*. New York: Pantheon Books.

Gonzalez , N., Moll, L., & Amanti, C. (2005). *Funds of knowledge: Theorizing practices in households, communications*. New York: Erlbaum.

Gonzalez, N. (2008). What is culture? In Rosebery, A. S., & Warren, B. (Eds.), *Teaching science to English learners: Building on students' strengths* (pp. 89–98). Arlington, VA: National Science Teachers Association.

Greenberg, J.B. (1989, April). Funds of knowledge: Historical constitution, social distribution, and transmission. Paper presented at the Annual Meeting of the Society for Applied Anthropology, Santa Fe, NM.

Henze, R. C., & Hauser, M. E. (1999). *Personalizing culture through anthropological and educational perspectives*. Santa Cruz, CA: Center for Research on Education, Diversity and Excellence.

Hymes, D. H. (1966). Two types of linguistic relativity. In Bright, W. (Ed.), *Sociolinguistics: Proceedings of the UCLA sociolinguistics conference 1964* (pp. 114–158). The Hague: Mouton.

Hymes, D. H. (1972). On communicative competence. In Pride, J. B., & Holmes, J. (Eds.), *Sociolinguistics: Selected readings* (pp. 269–293). Baltimore: Penguin.

Mosier, C. E., & Rogoff, B. (2003). Privileged treatment of toddlers: Cultural aspects of individual choice and responsibility. *Developmental Psychology, 39*(6), 1047.

Velez-Ibanez, C., & Greenberg, J. (1992). Formation and transformation of funds of knowledge among U.S. Mexican households. *Anthropology and Education Quarterly, 23*(4), 313–335.

2

• • • • •

Linguistic Anthropology + Sociolinguistics = The Ethnography of Communication

Now that we've had a chance to briefly discuss anthropology and ethnography, we need to focus in on the kind of ethnography that is the center of our concern. That is the ethnography of communication, and, as noted earlier, it has much in common with the field of sociolinguistics as well as the field of linguistic anthropology. Let's take a brief look at how this relationship began.

Ethnographers of communication study a uniquely human phenomenon—language as it is used to structure human behavior. Language influences and expresses human thought, and represents the knowledge possessed and needed to participate in communities of practice. Ferdinand de Saussure (1959) talked about the difference between *langue*—what you know about language rules—and *parole*—how you use language. Noam Chomsky built on Saussure's distinction, retheorizing it as a distinction between **competence** and **performance**. Both Saussure and Chomsky thought we should focus on *langue*/competence. Chomsky (1965) said that human beings are unique in being able to "generate an indefinitely large number of structures" (pp. 15–16). That's what competence is—our abstract understanding of "the rules of the road" for the language(s) we speak. Many people have the experience of learning explicitly about the rules of their native language when they study another language.

Thinking Together

Work in a small group.

Think about *langue*/competence (the rules of language that we are aware of and that are below our consciousness). As we learn languages, all of us overgeneralize the rules. English-speaking children say "three mouses" instead of "three mice" because they know the rule for plurals in English (i.e., add -*s* or -*es*), but they don't know there are exceptions. They say it, even though they never hear it from adults.

Come up with a list of things you have heard children or adult language learners say that show they are grappling with the rules of a language. Feel free to explore whatever languages you know (not just English). The way to find these is to think about exceptions to the rules. Here's a Spanish example: Saying "el mano" shows that you know the general rule that words ending in -*o* are usually masculine. But it's an exception, so it's "la mano". Come up with five examples.

Share your list with the whole class.

Because Chomsky's linguistic approach was built around language in the abstract and not in real-life practice, some people (Judy, Char, and lots of other people) see his theory as limited. Hymes responded to Chomsky's ideas, saying that scholars should also think about language use in its cultural and social contexts. Hymes argued that it's not either competence *or* performance, but rather it's competence *and* performance. He called the combination of these two ideas **communicative competence**. Communicative competence is what you know about and what you can do with a language. We are communicatively competent in our **communities of practice**.

Communities of practice, a concept first articulated by Lave and Wenger (1991), are groups of people who share social practices. Those practices involve language, symbols, and **multiple modalities**. Multiple modalities expand on speaking, listening, reading, and writing, to include spatial and gestural practices (Kalantzis and Cope, 2012). Communities of practice are about social practices and language practices. The ways people in a community of practice use language are marked far more by diversity than sameness. Language use is always affected by our social and cultural environments.

Linguistic anthropologists aren't so crazy about the *langue/parole* and competence/performance distinctions that Saussure and Chomsky came up with. Some people say we should think only about language use, or performance/*parole*. Hymes wanted to look at both competence and performance equally. He wanted us to focus on language use and social behavior by real people in everyday life, with the idea that our competence is also always there. Therefore, Hymes (1972/1986) suggested that we zero in on "[t]he interaction of language with social life . . . a matter of human action, based on a knowledge, sometimes conscious, often unconscious, that enables persons to use language" (p. 53). He reminded us that we have to expect and accept the natural variation that exists within language use and social practices.

Linguistic anthropologists and sociolinguists agree that all languages are composed of five aspects. To have communicative competence, you need to possess competence and demonstrate appropriate performance in all five. Linguistic anthropologists and sociolinguists emphasize the last two parts, semantics and pragmatics.

1. Morphology

Dr. Banner *morphs* into the Incredible Hulk when he gets angry. That is, he changes form. Morphology is the study of word formation. In English, we put prefixes at the beginning of words (a *re*run of *The Hulk* is on), suffixes at the end (uh-oh, the Hulk is chang*ing* again).

2. Phonology

Think about the word *telephone*. The *phon-* part of the word *phonology* has to do with sounds. Phonology is the study of the sound systems of languages. In sign language, it's about hand shape, position, and movement.

3. Syntax

Think about the word *sin*. Just kidding. There's no relationship between *sin* and *syn-*. Syntax is the study of how we put words and phrases together. It's a fancy word for grammar.

What follows are the most relevant aspects of language for us, because they are most directly embedded and embodied in the social world.

4. Semantics

Seme- is a Greek root that means *sign*. Semantics is the study of how people produce meaning by using language or other signs. We do this in the social world. Even if you have a particular personal/family meaning for something, it's still part of the social world. For example, Char has some friends who are a lesbian couple with a son. Their son calls one mom "Mama" and the other mom "Puma" or "Poohma" (after Winnie the Pooh). Puma/ Poohma, meaning other mom, was a word they needed where there wasn't an established one.

5. *Pragmatics*

Pragmatics is the study of practical, everyday language used by people in real communities of practice. It can overlap with semantics, but it's not just about how you use words in a social context. It's also about the culturally and socially appropriate ways we use language in particular settings (e.g., telling stories, giving speeches, having a conversation, etc. . . .). Here's an example: In Mexico, it's common for parents to give children advice in the form of *dichos*, or sayings/learnings. A popular one is, "El que habla dos lenguas vale por dos" (The person who speaks two languages is worth two people).

Thinking Together

Work in small groups.

What are some examples of making meaning socially and linguistically that you can think of, based on your own lives? Think about the Puma/ Poohma and the *dicho* examples. Come up with a list of five of your own.

Share your list with the class.

● ● ● ● ●

Ethnography of Communication

So our idea, that linguistic anthropological perspectives + socio-linguistic perspectives = ethnography of communication, isn't a traditional way of thinking about it, but we think it makes sense. We understand communication to include language (of course), but we don't stop at language. Communication happens through so many means. It includes the styles of clothes you wear, visual images, styles of music, and so on. Communication encompasses all of the **social projects** with which we are engaged. Do you skateboard? Go to protests against police brutality? Play in a band? Have a study group for a class? Belong to a running club? Get together with friends to watch movies? Attend services at a mosque/synagogue/church/temple? Those are social projects.

In any of your social projects, it's likely that you understand what other people are communicating and that they understand you. Even if you communicate creatively and with great personal flair, the fact that people understand you means that your communicative competence isn't completely unique. Trying to understand people's language use and their social practices in a community of practice is how we think of the ethnography of communication approach.

We've defined communication with a big C—Communication in its broadest terms—it's not just language but all signs and social projects. But what about ethnography? Whenever Char mentions to people that she's an ethnographer, they almost always look confused. *Ethnography* is not exactly a common word. But it's easy enough to think through. *Ethnos* = culture and *graphy* = writing. Ethnography is about writing culture. But, of course, it's not *just* about recording everything people say and do. Ethnographers aren't human surveillance cameras (with sound recording). Rather, ethnography is about observing and interpreting human behavior in particular sociocultural landscapes. It's about trying to comprehend how people understand themselves and about offering ways for them and for others to understand their practices in relation to social theory. But the idea of understanding others and representing them through words and/or images is highly complex.

● ● ● ● ●
The Revolution in Ethnography

Something big happened in 1986. No, it wasn't Whitney Houston recording "The Greatest Love of All", although that was important. It was the **reflective turn**, or what is also called the **postmodern turn** in anthropology. As in all intellectual revolutions, its ideas had been brewing for a while (Kuhn, 1962). The reflexive turn has its foundation in the 1960s, when the social movements of civil rights (for African-Americans, Chicanos, Native Americans, Asian Americans, and others), women's rights, and gay rights led anthropologists, as well as the people they studied, to question how powerful people represent less-powerful people. Before the 1960s, researchers didn't think much about how they wrote up their field notes and interviews. They saw observing people as just like observing animals and plants in nature. You write down what you see, and everyone who is there would see the same thing. Right? Not exactly.

New ways of thinking, spurred by the civil rights movements, powerfully impacted the social sciences. In his book *Reflections on Fieldwork in Morocco* (1977), Paul Rabinow questioned the role of anthropology in colonial projects. Feminist anthropologists like Ruth Behar, who wrote *Translated Woman: Crossing the Border with Esperanza's Story* (2003), pointed out that when women include themselves in the story, their work is often discounted. Native people, whom anthropologists had been staring at for a long time, were organizing the Red Power movement and taking back their power in relation to the stories told about them (Medicine, 2001).

These ideas came together in an influential way back in 1986 in a volume edited by James Clifford and George Marcus called *Writing Culture: The Poetics and Politics of Ethnography*. The essays in *Writing Culture* argued that ethnographic writing isn't a simple, transparent look into an objective world that everyone agrees on. They analyzed the role of power and rhetoric in ethnographic writing, critiquing the ways anthropologists produced authority and used storytelling techniques to make their work convincing. Clifford and Marcus made it clear that understanding other people is messy. A major takeaway from their work is that you can't just record what you see and hear in the social world and think of it as transparent. Your role in the sociocultural landscape impacts what you see. And how you tell the story is never a simple reporting of "the facts". Marcus and Fisher (1986) noted that our job now is to "reflect upon the practice of ethnography and the concept of culture" (p. 60). What you think is important and what you think isn't important are part of your interpretation. The way you organize and tell the story is interpretation. There is no clear, transparent meaning that emanates from the social world. Everything is mediated.

Some anthropologists saw *Writing Culture* as the book that discredited anthropology as a legitimate science. But many others (the majority in linguistic and cultural anthropology) have taken up the mantle of reflexivity, reflecting on their own role in the stories they tell and reimagining ethnography as a way of collaborating with people on research projects in communities of practice.

⊚ ⊚ ⊚ ⊚ ⊚

What Is Ethnography Now?

As of 2014, most ethnographic work will do more than just describe practices and analyze data in relation to social theory. It will involve researcher reflexivity, a privileging of the participants' perspectives, and often a political commitment to the group(s) being studied. For too long, ethnographers have pretended that their role didn't matter and have tried to erase their own power and privilege in the sharing of ethnographic knowledge. An analysis and understanding of how the dynamics of power play out in particular contexts are essential now. So is collaboration with the people being studied, which sometimes means conducting projects that matter to communities (McCarty,

2002) and sometimes means participants becoming co-authors (Cammorota and Fine, 2008).

Listening and Thinking About Positionality

Get into groups that are diverse for your context.

   Listen carefully to each person as they respond to these questions. It may help to use a talking stick (e.g., an object like a pencil or a water bottle) to make clear who holds the floor. Don't interrupt the person who has the floor.

1. Has your life been affected by race in any way? If yes, how? If not, why not?

2. Has your life been affected by gender and sexuality in any way? If yes, how? If not, why not?

3. Has your life been affected by your physical abilities in any way? If yes, how? If not, why not?

4. Has the "War on Terror" affected your social interactions in any way? If yes, how? If not, why not?*

   Go back to the whole group and share the highlights of what you've learned.

* Questions have been adapted from the work of Kaufman (2013).

● ● ● ● ●

Insider/Outsider Ethnography

We've just discussed how much ethnography has changed since the 1980s. Another way it has changed is with the idea of **insider/outsider ethnography**. It used to be that anthropologists thought understanding came from the fact that the ethnographer was an outsider to the community being studied. They thought the need to ask questions and make things explicit for the ethnographer who didn't know the social context was what produced knowledge. People don't believe that anymore. What does it mean to be an insider? What does it mean to be an outsider?

   These are complicated questions. Many times the people with whom we are conducting research make decisions about our degrees of insiderness and outsiderness. However, rather than thinking of these roles in a dichotomous way, it makes sense to think of them on a continuum. You might think that an insider is the best person to understand what's going on. Sometimes yes, sometimes no. It can happen that an insider is the ideal person to study a community of practice. But there are people who are very involved in their practices who don't want to analyze them. There are other people who aren't emotionally or intellectually connected to their communities of practice. And sometimes an outsider is the one who is curious and connected. It just depends. Both insiders and outsiders can gain important insights about a community and share those insights with the community and scholarly communities.

Michéle Foster (2010) has written about the complexities of doing research in her own community. In her life-history project about Black teachers, Foster was put through tests by the participants in her study, to prove to them that she was Black enough for them to recount their experiences to. At the same time, an elder who had taught for more than 50 years in a one-room schoolhouse told her, "I've been waiting a long time for somebody Black to come hear my story" (p. 394).

Sofia Villenas (2010) has reflected on the complexities of having aspects of your identity read by other people in ways you don't want. While conducting a study about family literacy practices in a Latin@ community in North Carolina, Villenas found that the White program administrators positioned her as one of them because of her educational background. At the same time, they vilified the Latin@ participants in the family literacy program, seeing them as deficient parents. Villenas related more to the Latina mothers she worked with, and she had to fight the administrators' assumptions that she held the same views they did.

The reality is that all of us have multiple identities, and we are often simultaneously insiders in one sense and outsiders in another. Because we are researchers, that almost always makes us outsiders in one way, regardless of our other identities. Communications scholars Naaeke, Kurylo, Grabowski, Linton, and Radford (2012) reflected on the insider/outsider dichotomy this way:

> *Particularly, the terms are slippery. We don't necessarily know in which way we might be perceived as an insider or outsider because we all have multiple group identities and shift among these in each moment depending on which ones are salient in a certain interaction. One's insider or outsider status changes even in interactions with the same people and even in the same conversations. To treat a researcher as either one or the other is to assume these are static.*
>
> *(p. 158)*

And we love the example given in this same article by communications scholar Michael Grabowski, who studies how people talk about menstruation. Although he doesn't menstruate (wink), he considers himself an insider, because men have mostly controlled the discourse about menstruation. This is an interesting twist, isn't it? It comes from an awareness of power relationships.

Thinking Together

Work in a small group.

Think about yourself as a student in this class. This class is a community of practice, right? Where do you think you fall on the insider/outsider continuum? Mark your continuum without showing it to the people in your group. Now, have them decide where you are on the continuum. Are your perceptions the same? Different? Why?

Your insider/outsider status:

Insider ——————————————————————————— Outsider

Your classmates' evaluation of your insider/outsider status:

Insider ——————————————————————————— Outsider

● ● ● ● ●

The Emic/Etic Distinction

Have you ever heard the terms **emic** and **etic**? Historically, these concepts grew out of linguistics and later anthropology, but they are used in many fields today. You may have seen them in other subject areas, such as psychology, folklore, medicine, nursing, public health, education, psychiatry, sociology, education, and even business. These concepts get around.

Linguist Kenneth Pike coined the terms emic/etic a long time ago (Pike, 1954/1967). They come from the Greek roots of the concepts phon**emic** and phon**etic**. He thought of emic as the knowledge a cultural group (or a community of practice) has about their world. Emic knowledge is the kind of knowledge that it might take the outsider ethnographer a while to understand, and that the insider ethnographer might take for granted. Pike thought of etic as the formalized knowledge that comes from emic perspectives that would be connected to larger social theories and that gets published. An emic perspective is a folk theory that has a particular meaning in a sociocultural group. An etic perspective is an academic theory, something that has been defined formally. Some people call it the insider/outsider distinction, but that's not really it. It's more about steps in the process of collecting and analyzing ethnographic data.

Back in the 1950s, Pike was thinking a lot about whether linguistic knowledge was subjective or objective. That was in the days when social scientists modeled their work on that of chemists and biologists, and **positivism** was the dominant way of thinking. Positivism is the foundation of the scientific method, and it is the belief that knowledge comes only from observable, measurable facts that are verifiable. Positivists believe that if something is true in one context, it is true in all contexts. Even back in the heyday of positivism, Pike understood that it wasn't possible for him to describe a language objectively. He knew his positionality impacted what he saw. For him, the problem was that as an outsider, he couldn't understand what it was that insiders knew about their languages until he had been there a long time, and even then he saw that what he could know was limited.

Anthropologist Marvin Harris (1976, 1980) made the concepts emic/etic popular in anthropology, and he focused on using the emic/etic distinction to look at social behavior, whereas Pike focused on language use. Harris was working hard to figure out the epistemological status of the things participants told him. Were they true? False? Both? Something else entirely? Harris used emic to mean the ways people understood and talked about their lives, their behavior, and their beliefs. He used etic to refer to the ways the emic perspective is understood in the academic literature. He saw both emic and etic knowledge as equally important and as stages in ethnographic understanding.

Think about this: Among Mexican and Mexican-American people, it's common to experience a kind of fright illness from sudden shock. Some people believe that the soul is shocked out of the body and can't get back in. This is called *susto*. It can be debilitating, even life-threatening. It might happen as the result of the death of a loved one, but it can really be caused by anything. The way people usually heal from it is through the rituals of a *curander@*. Western physicians often think of the symptoms of *susto* as mapping onto depression or post-traumatic stress disorder. This is a classic example of emic and etic knowledge. Baer and Bustillo (1993) have written about *susto* among farmworkers in Florida, and they argue that while the symptoms of *susto* don't line up exactly with the Western medicine categories of disease, both approaches are real. They suggest that physicians acknowledge that folk diagnoses are about real illnesses, and they urge folk healers to consider that biomedical approaches might also be used effectively to heal them.

Hymes (1970) also addressed how sometimes the emic point of view is difficult to articulate. That's usually because it's below our consciousness, and we don't think to talk about it until someone asks. Even when someone asks, it can be difficult to figure out why we do what we do and think what we think.

Reflecting Together

Linguistic anthropologist Jane Hill studied emic perspectives (folk theories) about racism among White people in the United States (2008). She found this to be a popular folk theory about race among White people:

> Although race is biologically real, and everyone belongs to a race, over time, intermarriage will cause racial differences to diminish. "Thus, racism will disappear by itself, since there will be no differences left for racists to notice."
>
> (p. 6)

Work in diverse groups for your context. Listen carefully to your classmates as they talk. Use a talking stick (e.g., a pencil, a water bottle) to give each person the floor.
What is your folk theory about racism?

You might be wondering about the relationship between insider/outsider ethnographers and emic/etic perspectives. Can only insider ethnographers understand emic perspectives? Can only outsider ethnographers have etic perspectives? Scholars agree that emic knowledge can be understood by both insiders and outsiders, and that etic perspectives can be developed by both insiders and outsiders.

● ● ● ● ●

Ethnocentrism

We have been talking about the continuum of insider/outsider status. This leads us to the idea of **ethnocentrism**, which is the idea that the way you were taught to do things and to understand the world is the best way to understand the world. Another way to say it is as follows:

Ethnocentrism can be viewed as having three levels: positive, negative, *and* extremely negative. *The first,* positive, *is the belief that, at least for you, your culture is preferred over all others. This is natural, and inherently there is nothing wrong with it because you draw much of your personal identity and many of your beliefs from your native culture. At the* negative *level, you partially take on a evaluative dimension. You believe your culture is the center of everything and all other cultures should be measured and rated by its standards. . . . Finally, in the* extreme negative *form, it is not enough to consider your culture as the most valid and useful; you also perceive your culture to be the most powerful one, and even believe that your values and beliefs should be adopted by other cultures.*

(Samovar, Porter, and McDaniel, 2010, p. 180)

Talking Together

Your class will watch an excerpt from the film *My Big Fat Greek Wedding*, at http://www.youtube.com/watch?v=WPvO53JHnmY

What do you think is happening in this scene? Is ethnocentrism going on here? For whom? Does it fit into the categories of positive, negative, or extremely negative? Why? Give examples.

The Sacred Rac

Read this brief ethnographic report: http://www.abstractconcreteworks.com/essays/teaching/Composition-111/70-c-sacred-rac.html

Now, answer these questions:

1. Who are the Asu?
2. What is their rac?
3. How does this article lead you to reevaluate your knowledge and expectations?
4. Would you date an Asu person? Why or why not?
5. Do you think your family would accept an Asu person? Why or why not?

Common metaphors such as wearing another person's hat or walking in someone else's shoes are used to convey the idea that it is not easy to understand others' ways of life or ways of viewing the world. In the ethnographic context, this metaphor allows us to understand the concept of ethnocentrism—the view that your own culture or community is at the center of all others and therefore is the logical foundation from which to attempt to understand all other cultures and communities. In other words, ethnocentrism is attempting to understand what others do in the context and with the knowledge of what you do. This most often fails to produce an accurate understanding because you end up interpreting others through your own lens.

● ● ● ● ●

Wrapping Up

In this chapter, we have explored the foundations of the ethnography of communication—a foundation that has both blended and developed with the disciplines of anthropology and linguistics. As we continue to develop your foundation in the discipline and prepare you for your own ethnographic fieldwork, we move next to a discussion of the role of social theory in the ethnography of communication.

This article and others that appear in various chapters as examples of ethnographic inquiry can be accessed through your university library, and the information you need to search for them is available in the References section at the end of this chapter:

● ● ● ● ●

References

Baer, R. D., & Bustillo, M. (1993). Susto and mal de ojo among Florida farmworkers: EMIC and ETIC perspectives. *Medical Anthropology Quarterly, 7,* 90–100.

Behar, R. (2003). *Translated woman: Crossing the border with Esperanza's story.* Boston: Beacon.

Cammarota, J., & Fine, M. (2008). Youth participatory action research: A pedagogy for transformational resistance. In Cammarota, J., & Fine, M. (Eds.), *Revolutionizing education: Youth participatory action research in motion* (pp. 1–11). New York: Routledge.

Chomsky, N. (1965). *Aspects of the theory of syntax.* Cambridge, MA: MIT Press.

Clifford, J., & Marcus, G. E. (Eds.). (1986). *Writing culture: The poetics and politics of ethnography* Berkeley, CA: University of California Press.

Foster, M. (2010). The power to know one thing is never the power to know all things: Methodological notes on two studies of Black American teachers. In Luttrell, W. (Ed.), *Qualitative educational research: Readings in reflexive methodology and transformative practice* (pp. 384–398). New York: Routledge.

Harris, M. (1976). History and significance of the emic/etic distinction. *Annual Review of Anthropology, 5,* 329–350.

Harris, M. (1980). Cultural materialism: The struggle for a science of culture. New York: Random House.

Hill, J. H. (2008). *The everyday language of white racism.* Malden, MA: Wiley-Blackwell.

Hughes, P. (1986). The sacred rac. Pp. 61-71. In S. Fersh (Ed.) Learning about Peoples and Cultures, Evanston, IL: MacDougall Littell.

Hymes, D. (1970). On communicative competence. In J. J. Gumperz and D. Hymes (eds). *Directions in Sociolinguistics.* New York: Holt, Rinehart and Winston.

Hymes, D. (1972/1986). Models of the interaction of language and social life. In Gumperz, J. J., & Hymes, D. (Eds.), *Directions in sociolinguistics: The ethnography of communication* (pp. 35–71). Oxford: Blackwell.

Kalantzis, M., and Cope, B. (2012). *Literacies.* Cambridge: Cambridge University Press.

Kaufman, P. (2013). Scribo ergo cogito: Reflexivity through writing. *Teaching Sociology, 41*(1), 70–81.

Kuhn, T. S. (1962). *The Structure of Scientific Revolutions* (1st ed.). University of Chicago Press.

Lave, J., & Wenger, E. (1991). *Situated learning: Legitimate peripheral participation.* New York: Cambridge University Press.

Marcus, G. E., & Fischer, M. M. J. (1986). *Anthropology as cultural critique: An experimental moment in the human sciences.* Chicago: University of Chicago Press.

McCarty, T. L. (2002). *A place to be Navajo: Rough Rock and the struggle for self-determination in indigenous schooling.* New York: Routledge.

Medicine, B. (2001). My elders tell me. In Medicine, B., and Jacobs, S. (Eds.), *Learning to be an anthropologist and remaining "native": Selected writings* (pp. 73–82). Urbana: University of Illinois Press.

Naaeke, A., Kurylo, A., Grabowski, M., Linton, D., and Radford, M. (2012). Insider and outsider perspective in ethnographic research. *Proceedings of the New York State Communication Association*, 152–160.

Pike, K. (1954/1967). *Language in relation to a unified theory of structure of human behavior.* The Hague: Mouton.

Rabinow, P. (1977). *Reflections on fieldwork in Morocco.* Berkeley: University of California Press.

Samovar, L. A., Porter, R. E., & McDaniel, E. R. (2010). *Communication between cultures.* Boston: Wadsworth.

Saussure, F. de. (1959). The nature of the linguistic sign. In *Course in General Linguistics* (pp. 65–70). New York: McGraw-Hill.

Villenas, S. (2010). Thinking Latina/o education with and from Chicana/Latina feminist cultural studies. In Z. Leonardo (Ed.), *Handbook of cultural politics in education* (pp. 454–479). Boston: Sense.

3

●●●●●

Using Social Theory

You may be saying to yourself, "Wait a minute. I thought I would be a participant observer in a community and that I was going to listen carefully to the ways people use language. I didn't sign up for theory. And *social* theory? Uh-oh." We understand. Many people get nervous when they hear the word *theory*. But theory can be very useful, and we plan to demonstrate that to you. We hope that reading this chapter will help demystify theory for you.

●●●●●

What Is Theory?

Have you ever wondered why social worlds work the way they do? If so, you have asked a question you can use **social theory** to understand. The goal of theory is to improve your understanding of the world. Think about theory as a pair of glasses that help you see better. Let's take that vision metaphor a bit further: while some of us wear glasses or contacts, all of us (for the most part) have lenses in our eyes. Those lenses in our eyes are a way of understanding the world. They are our personal theories. But if we use glasses, the world comes into even sharper focus. Different theories are like different glasses, and they can bring many things to light that we simply couldn't see before.

Different Uses of the Term

You may be feeling confused by this way of thinking about theory. If you have studied the physical or natural sciences, theory is used differently in those contexts. There, it's about explaining and predicting behavior. In its purest form, this approach is called positivism, an idea we talked about in Chapter 2. If a theory explains and predicts behavior in one place, it is expected to work the same way everywhere. Airplanes follow the laws of thermodynamics the same way in every country of the world, right? Why shouldn't the social world work the same way? Well . . . we believe it's not possible to map that approach to the physical world onto the social world and assume everything is the same. Our social worlds have different norms, practices, and ideologies, and our languages and cultures are highly contextual. Social theory is different from other kinds of theory. It's even different from sociological theory, which has adopted a more positivist approach, as you will see.

Historically, the ethnography of communication approach developed on a different track from the field of social theory. We understand **social theory** as coming from hermeneutics (Gadamer, 2004), a field of inquiry that focuses on how people make meanings through spoken language but also through multiple modalities, such as writing, visual media, and art. While Gadamer and Hymes shared a fascination with the ways people use spoken language, Hymes (1972) was influenced by the positivist framework. He saw sociolinguistic fieldwork as an essential part of moving the field toward structural and generative "models of sociolinguistic description, formulation of universal sets of features and relations, and explanatory theories" (p. 43). He wanted the ethnography of communication approach to become more and more about explanation and universal applicability.

Levinson et al. (2011) make a useful distinction between social theory and sociological theory. They see sociological theory as emphasizing explanation and generalizability, and social theory, in contrast, as about interpreting the world. They suggest that using social theory is a way to "enrich and extend the analytic power of everyday *ours* social theories" (p. 7). That is, social theory can build on our personal and collective understandings of the world and help us to imagine even better worlds. Wendy Brown (quoted in Levinson et al, 2011, p. 7) says, "theory does not simply decipher the meanings of the world, but recodes and rearranges them in order to reveal something about the meanings and incoherencies we live with" (p. 7). That means social theories, in conversation with our personal and cultural explanations of the world, help us to look at our own theories, so that we can see them differently and perhaps create social change.

We all live in social worlds. Even if you're a hermit and you are reading this book, you are engaged in a social interaction. Biology is part of the social world; chemistry is part of the social world—it's not as if there are all the messy social sciences, and then "real" science is separate somehow. There is no outside of the social world. All of us strive to make meaning out of our lives, and meaning making is on a continuum between our own individual understandings and the social theory that helps us see larger social processes and possible worlds. Social theory is about increased understanding, not explanation. Reinventing the ethnography of communication approach for the 21st century and beyond means incorporating social theory as a means of understanding language data from the social world.

● ● ● ● ●

Framing the Ethnography of Communication

What is the relationship between social theory and the empirical data we gather in the ethnography of communication? We see our data and social theory as part of a constant conversation about what the world means. The contexts that are part of all social happenings are where our knowledge comes from. That is, we build knowledge through this back-and-forth conversation between everyday behaviors in their particular contexts and social theory. What we are saying is that the relationship between theory and data is reciprocal.

We encourage you to read widely in social theory, and we will end this chapter with lots of recommendations for you to explore. We don't want you to stop with our recommendations but rather to use them as a springboard to find new thinkers and new ideas. We do have a piece of advice as you venture out into the world of social theory. Don't become a disciple of any particular theory (at least at the beginning), and stay open to new possibilities. Dressman (2008) suggests that using multiple social theories to understand your data is a way of maintaining a critical stance toward theory and not being overly influenced by any one way of thinking. He says we always need to ask how a theory might NOT explain our data. This is a great way to use social theory.

Have you ever heard the phrase, "When you have a hammer, everything looks like a nail"? In 1964 Abraham Kaplan was credited with this idea, which he called the law of the instrument. Later Maslow (1966), the psychologist, elaborated on it, and it became popularized. What does it mean? Think of a theory as a tool. When you find a new tool, you want to try it out everywhere. Suddenly, you are single-minded, and you risk overgeneralizing a new theory.

Char remembers when she became aware of a particular color that was mildly popular in women's clothing a few years ago. It's a color that's hard to describe—it's a kind of green with a lot of yellow in it—it sort of looks like very green olive oil with light shining through it. When she noticed it and decided she liked it, the color began to jump out at her. When she was in a crowd, it was as if the people wearing that color had arrows around them. Her attention was pulled to that new awareness.

Thinking Together

Work with a partner.
    Think about the new-instrument theory. Have you had an experience of becoming aware of something new and suddenly seeing it everywhere? Describe it.
    Share your experiences with the whole class.

While those new-instrument experiences eventually fade away in our perceptual worlds, they can be pesky for us as researchers. If you fall in love with a particular theory, then it only allows you to see certain things in your data. There is no room for new understandings or for finding things in your data that you didn't expect already. Sometimes, people are even tempted to use the theory that they believe in so strongly as a stand-in for data. That's a problem.

Here's an example. Early in her doctoral program, Char had read a lot of Marx and Engels (1978), Marx (1998) and Bowles and Gintis (1976). Not long after that, she started teaching English to Speakers of Other Languages (ESOL) at an adult school where most of the students were undocumented migrants, which is where she ended up conducting her dissertation research. It would have been easy for her to understand her students' lives as all structure and no agency, based on the theory she had been reading. But the more she spent time with her students, the more she realized that while those theories allowed her to see structural oppression, they didn't allow her to see agency. While she continued to see the ways in which the lives of undocumented people were profoundly limited by structural constraints, she also saw the complex ways in which people used language, the ways in which they dealt with the border patrol, and many other examples of their agency. Her study participants made it clear that they saw being able to study English as an act of agency. Learning English was a way to protect themselves from workplace abuses, even if it didn't always work out that way. But the reality was that both things were true.

We encourage you to read social theory before you begin to collect data, but to hold off on reading too much theory while you are in the field. We don't want you to miss seeing everything you can possibly see. Try to listen to that voice in the back of your head that keeps asking, "How does this theory NOT explain my data?" Sometimes you will read a theory that helps you to see new things in your data. When that happens, it's exciting. Remember, you are trying on different glasses all the time. One pair allows you to see one thing, and another pair allows you to see something that wasn't even visible when you were wearing the other glasses. There is no single theory, no perfect pair of glasses, that makes it possible for you to see everything at once. That's why we have to keep trying on glasses/theories.

Dressman (2008) has two axioms for social science researchers that we think you should know about. They are essential to doing the ethnography of communication.

● ● ● ● ●

Axiom 1: Data Never Speaks for Itself

What does this mean? Well, first of all, language is not transparent; it's refractive. That is, language is not a neutral phenomenon. It refracts meanings as much as it clarifies them. Dressman also means that no matter how careful you are to become aware of your schemata, your own "values and the fact that all prior knowledge is only partial always affect the production of what counts as knowledge" (Dressman, 2008, p. 57). Researchers frequently find what they set out to find. Is that a coincidence? Probably not. Dressman argues, and we agree with him, that all knowledge is necessarily provisional and unfinished. Our claims as to what it's possible to know are more humble than they were in the modernist era of 'objectivity'.

We would like you to remember the idea that "data never speaks for itself" as you conduct your study and, at the same time, when you are ready to sit down to write. Scribble "data never speaks for itself" on a Post-It note, and abide by it as you write. You need to guide the reader to your interpretation of the data, and you do that with theory. Don't think that you can just include lots of quotes and not interpret them. Data never speaks for itself. You have to tell your reader how you are interpreting your data.

● ● ● ● ●

Axiom 2: Doing Social Research Is a Rhetorical Activity

This axiom may be shocking if you come from a background where you were taught that it's possible to know and understand the world completely. But we believe that this is true of all research, not just social science research. Dressman (2008) asks us to consider the rhetorical techniques of a traditional quantitative study. Researchers might use the third person and the passive voice (It was found . . .) to distance themselves from the research, a strategy to make the study seem objective. They might spend a lot of time explaining their methods, to encourage the reader to see the study as valid and to assume that the conclusions are obviously true, because of the validity of the methods.

Analyzing Together

Work in small groups. Each person will get online and download a different peer-reviewed ethnographic study from your school library (if you have the database Anthrosource, that's a good place to start).

What are the rhetorical techniques that the researcher used? Discuss the techniques you see in your group, and then share what you learned with the class.

All of us communicate with rhetorical techniques and tropes. Don't think it's a bad thing. There is no other way to do it. Because we have lived in a positivist-influenced moment for quite a while, we haven't always noticed the tropes that are the norms in more traditionally scientific writing. But the idea was for us not to notice them.

In this postmodern, interpretive moment, many researchers have turned away from the search for universals and the unreconstructed use of grand theory that explains all of human behavior (think of people like Marx and Freud). Instead, they have turned toward postmodern, postmodern-feminist, post-colonial, and critical race theorists whose work embraces complexity, multiple discourses, processes, and the local. The list of theorists whose work we encourage you to explore leans toward those who might help you understand relations of power. Why? Because power relations are continually constructing and being constructed by language practices.

When you start reading social theory, you need to look for theories that help you make sense of your data. That's essential. But you also have to think about your audience. Which journals publish empirical studies that use those theories or might be open to those theories? Just as you will learn to be a participant observer in the community you study, you will also learn to become a participant in a particular scholarly discourse community. How do they talk? How do they think? You have to find the right group to join, so that sharing your data and your interpretation makes sense to them. We don't mean that you shouldn't explore new theoretical approaches. You should do that. What we mean is that your exciting new ways of thinking need to be expressed so that your audience can understand them.

●●●●●
Where Do I Begin?

In this section, we present you with some social theorists who think about issues of language and power, and whose work is likely to help you interpret the data you gather in your ethnography of communication study. All of them have been widely influential for people who think about language use. Our list is more eclectic than comprehensive, but it will get you started. Don't feel tied to this list, by any means.

1. Gloria Anzaldúa was a scholar of Chicana, feminist, and queer theory. She lived from 1942 to 2004.

    Big ideas: mestizaje, hybridity, borders, borderlands

    Recommended reading:

    Anzaldúa, G. (1987). *Borderlands/La Frontera: The new mestiza.* San Francisco: Aunt Lute Books.

Keating, A. L. (Ed.). (2009). *The Gloria Anzaldúa reader.* Durham, NC: Duke University Press.

2. Arjun Appadurai is an anthropologist whose work looks at modernity and globalization. He was born in 1949.

   Big ideas: social imaginary (ethnoscapes, mediascapes, technoscapes, financescapes, ideoscapes)

   Recommended reading:

   Appadurai, A. (Ed.). (2002). *Globalization.* Durham, NC: Duke University Press.

   Appadurai, A. (1996). *Modernity at large: Cultural dimensions of globalization.* Minneapolis: University of Minnesota Press.

3. Mikhail Bakhtin was a Russian philosopher and semiotician. He lived from 1895 to 1975.

   Big ideas: heteroglossia, polyphony, authoritative discourse, centripetal and centrifugal force, carnival, dialogism, hybrid

   Recommended reading:

   Bakhtin, M. M. (1981). *The dialogic imagination.* C. Emerson and M. Holquist (Trans.). Austin: University of Texas Press.

   Voloshinov, V. N. (1973). *Marxism and the philosophy of language.* L. Matejka and I. R. Titunk (Trans.) Cambridge, MA: Harvard University Press. (Bakhtin published under Voloshinov's name sometimes.)

4. Homi K. Bhabha is a key figure in post-colonial theory. He was born in 1949.

   Big ideas: third space, hybridity, mimicry, ambivalence, difference, fixity

   Recommended reading:

   Bhabha, H. K. (2004). *The location of culture.* New York: Routledge.

   Bhabha, H. K. (1990). *Nation and narration.* New York: Routledge.

5. Pierre Bourdieu was a French sociologist. He lived from 1930 to 2002.

   Big ideas: practice, habitus, cultural capital, linguistic capital, field, doxa, social reproduction, distinction, symbolic violence

   Recommended reading:

   Bourdieu, P. (1977). *Outline of a theory of practice.* R. Nice (Trans.). Cambridge: Cambridge University Press.

   Bourdieu, P. (1994). *Language and symbolic power.* Cambridge, MA: Harvard University Press.

6. Judith Butler is a key figure in gender theory/queer theory whose work involves language. She was born in 1958.

Big ideas: performativity, the heterosexual matrix, gender melancholia, iteration, citationality, subjectivity

Recommended reading:

Butler, J. (2006). *Gender trouble: Feminism and the subversion of identity.* New York: Routledge.

Butler, J. (1997). *The psychic life of power: Theories in subjection.* New York: Routledge.

7. Michel Foucault was a French philosopher and historian whose work involves language, sexuality, and power. He lived from 1926 to 1984.

   Big ideas: discourse, discursive practice, the incitement to discourse, power/knowledge, governmentality, archaeology, genealogy, biopower, episteme, regimes of truth, discipline, problematization, resistance

   Recommended reading:

   Foucault, M. (1990). *A history of sexuality.* Vol. 1. A. Sheridan (Trans.). New York: Vintage.

   Foucault, M. (1995). *Discipline and punish: The birth of the prison.* A. Sheridan (Trans.). New York: Vintage.

8. Antonio Gramsci was an Italian Marxist theorist of politics and language. He lived from 1891 to 1937.

   Big ideas: hegemony, common sense, organic intellectual

   Recommended reading:

   Gramsci, A. (1971). *Selections from the prison notebooks.* T. Q. Hoare and G. N. Smith (Trans.). London: Wishart.

9. Henri Lefebvre was a French sociologist and philosopher. He lived from 1901 to 1991.

   Big ideas: the right to the city, everyday life, the production of social space

   Recommended reading:

   Lefebvre, H. (2008). *Critique of everyday life.* Vol. 1. New York: Verso.

   Lefebvre, H. (1992). *The production of social space.* New York: Wiley-Blackwell.

10. Gayati Chakravorty Spivak is an Indian philosopher and a key figure in post-colonial theory. She was born in 1942.

    Big ideas: subaltern, strategic essentialism, epistemological performance

Recommended reading:

Spivak, G. (1999). *A critique of post-colonial reason: Toward a history of the vanishing present.* Cambridge, MA: Harvard University Press.

Spivak, G., Landry, D. & MacLean, G. (Eds.). (1995). *The Spivak reader: Selected works of Gayatri Chakravorty.* New York: Routledge.

This article and others that appear in various chapters as examples of ethnographic inquiry can be accessed through your university library, and the information you need to search for them is available in the References section at the end of this chapter:

●●●●●
_____

References

Bowles, S., & Gintis, H. (1976). *Schooling in capitalist America: Educational reform and the contradictions of economic life.* New York: Basic Books.

Dressman, M. (2008). *Using social theory in educational research: A practical guide.* New York: Routledge.

Gadamer, H. (2004). *Truth and method.* (J. Weinsheimer & D. G. Marshall, Trans.). New York: Crossroad.

Hymes, D. (1972). Models of the interaction of language and social life. In Gumperz, J. J., & Hymes, D. (Eds.), *Directions in sociolinguistics: The ethnography of communication* (pp. 35–71). New York: Holt, Rinehart, & Winston.

Kaplan, A. (1964). *The conduct of inquiry: Methodology for behavioral science.* San Francisco: Chandler.

Levinson, B.A.U., with P.J. Gross, J. Heimer Dadds, C. Hanks, K. Kumasi, D. Metro-Roland, and J. Link. (2011). *Beyond Critique: Exploring Critical Social Theories and Education.* Boulder, CO: Paradigm Publishers.

Marx, K. (1998). *The German ideology.* New York: Prometheus Books.

Marx, K., & Engels, F. (1978). *The Marx/Engels reader* (2nd ed.). New York: Norton.

Maslow, A. H. (1966). *The psychology of science: A reconnaissance.* New York: Harper.

4

• • • • •

A Framework for Doing the Ethnography of Communication
Ethnography of Communication Redux

In this chapter, we rethink some of the assumptions about ethnography of communication, and then we work through our expansion of it step-by-step in the chapters that follow. We start with Hymes' idea of the ethnography of communication, an approach that has been foundational in sociolinguistics and a perspective in which Judy is well schooled. She also schooled Char in it, back in the day. While we respect, appreciate, and acknowledge the seismic change Hymes' work has caused in many academic fields of study (i.e., linguistics, anthropology, education, and communication studies, just to name a few), we also understand that, like everything, the field has grown. Hymes was a visionary back in the 1960s. He understood that people do and think important things with language(s) all the time. He showed us that it's possible to learn about the social world through careful and systematic attention to language use.

That's a great place to start. But it's our intention in this text to push Hymes' work a little further. One way we do this is by being explicit about the how-to part of his approach. Another way is by updating it theoretically. One of the critiques of the ethnography of communication approach has been that it doesn't connect to the world of social theory. Ethnography of Communication studies can end up producing detailed, thick-description accounts of language use about which people say, "So what?" By updating this approach with an understanding of postmodern theory and the positionality of knowledge, we will show you how the ethnography of communication can be relevant to our understandings of the world today.

Another way we are updating this approach is by understanding communication as part of something bigger than language. That is, the ethnography of communication approach is a way to understand all of the social projects in which we humans are engaged. It's COMMUNICATION, writ large.

⬤ ⬤ ⬤ ⬤ ⬤

Participant Observation

Let's think about what it might mean for us to be participant observers in the real world rather than in a laboratory. Genzuk (2003) explains that the observation and analysis of naturally occurring behavior are central to developing an understanding that grows inductively rather than deductively. **Deductive inquiry** begins with a set of hypothesis-testing experiments that stem from what the researcher expects to see as human beings act and interact. A **hypothesis** is a guess about what you think is going to happen. Because it's a guess, you don't know if it's true. That's why you test it.

Inductive inquiry works in just the reverse way. It begins with a general question or theme, and then the researchers do participant observation, conduct interviews, and collect artifacts. After gathering a lot of data, they start to see patterns emerge, and only then do they come to some conclusions. Inductive inquiry is about discovery, not prediction. Ethnography is typically an inductive process. So there we are, as ethnographers, immersing ourselves in communities. Don't we affect the people we are trying to understand, simply by being there? Of course, we do. But over time we develop relationships with the people with whom we are conducting research. And the researcher's identity locations (i.e., race, gender, class, sexuality, religious background, and on and on) impact what the researcher has access to and how the researcher interacts with the person being observed or interviewed.

In sociolinguistic research, people used to think about what Labov (1972) called the **observer's paradox**—that is, the need to find out what people do when the researcher isn't there. The paradox was that what you wanted to find out, you could never know unless you were there. There was an assumption that over time the researcher might come to have little or no impact on what was knowable, a belief that was tied to positivist notions of objectivity. That is, there was a belief that everything knowable could be observed and that the only limit to what we know was what we could not observe. Now, in this postmodern moment, researchers are more likely to see what is knowable as produced through interaction among the researcher and the participants in the study and the context.

● ● ● ● ●

Minimizing the Researcher's Impact

Along with trying to minimize the influence our presence can have on people, we need to listen to people carefully and respectfully and participate in community settings while postponing our judgments about people and what they do. The method of choice in the ethnography of communication is participant observation. There are two methods embedded in the name of the process itself. We participate in and observe the community we are studying. If we were only observing the community, we would have difficulty coming to understand the kind of insider knowledge people have that leads to their being members of a community of practice. But there are degrees of participation and of knowledge. People have different roles in various communities, and they have different kinds of power.

For example, although Char learned a lot about how a particular group of undocumented people navigated life in the United States at a particular moment in time in a particular place, she did not come to be an undocumented person in the United States. She still had a lot of privilege, given that she was born in the United States. In fact, legal status was just one aspect of her privilege, given that she's White, middle class, English dominant, and able-bodied. At the same time, she came to look at the world through the insights that undocumented people shared with her as a participant observer. She came to think of herself as both an insider and an outsider for that particular moment in time.

Some people question whether an outsider can understand a community in the same ways an insider can. Other people ask whether an insider can understand a community as well as an outsider. There's an old joke, where one fish swimming next to another fish says, "Isn't the water great today?" The other fish doesn't say anything. As it swims away, it thinks to itself, "What the heck is water?" Sometimes when you're an insider, it's hard to see your own group. It's true that insiders know too many things for outsiders to learn completely. At that same time, it's true that outsiders often see things that are below the consciousness of insiders.

As we mentioned in Chapter 3, people used to think that the only way to gather ethnographic data was to be a total outsider to the community you were studying. That is no longer how scholars think about this relationship. Rather, the central difference is that one person—the ethnographer—is conducting the study, and the others—the participants—are not. It's best to think of the insider-outsider relationship as a continuum rather than a binary. Whereever you fall on the insider/outsider continuance, you can produce important knowledge. It takes the insider part of the contiuum to produce the outsider part of the continuum, and vice versa. Ethnographic inquiry is a process of cooperative discovery. Both you and members of the community of practice will learn from this endeavor. Wherever you are on the insider-outsider continuum, both what you know and what you will learn through participant observation, interviewing, and artifact collection will inform how you collect and analyze data.

Reflecting on Your Insider/Outsider Status

Work with a partner.

What are some groups in which you are an insider? School? A religious group? A social group? On that old TV show *Cheers*, the folks who went to the bar every day were insiders at the bar, weren't they?

Are there groups in which you are a partial insider? What does it mean to participate in those groups?

Now think about what it might mean to systematically observe what's going on in a group that you participate in.

We believe that being a participant and an observer will give you a deeper understanding of a sociocultural landscape than being just a participant or just an observer.

What do you think?

Asking questions is not a practice that should be saved for any one part of the research process. Indeed, you need to ask questions whenever gaps in your knowledge arise. It may feel like that is all the time. Many times, you will record questions in your field notes that you cannot ask in the moment. Sometimes those questions will be answered through further observation. Other times, you will ask them directly. You have to work hard, though, not to interrupt people in their everyday lives and to minimize your intrusion. Sometimes that means not asking questions at a particular time; other times, it may mean jumping in to help with something.

Char remembers an informal conversation that happened while she was helping a participant take laundry off the clothesline. As the conversation continued, Char learned that this person knew that people in the village talked about her family. People said openly that her family was violent and that it wasn't OK. Char found out that this person had a feeling that other people didn't live the way she did, and she wanted to live more peacefully. She wanted her father to get sober. Because this person had never before acknowledged to Char that her father was alcoholic, this is the kind of thing she couldn't have asked about in a formal interview.

You never want to ask judgmental questions. You never want to challenge a participant's knowledge or actions. You want only to understand. We know that we change situations simply with our presence, but we want to make the impact of our being there minimal. Sometimes, as in Char's situation, this is best done through joining in and being part of the flow of life.

The ethnography of communication approach offers steps for us to follow from the point of selecting a community to research to the point of sharing our findings with others. Within this framework, we focus on a collaborative process for conducting research (Lassiter 2005). It's our hope that your research leads to praxis and that it's truly transformative. Praxis, according to Freire (2006), is "the reflection and action which truly transform reality, [and] is the source of knowledge and creation" (pp. 100–101). Sometimes an ethnographer's work is transformative for the participants, the larger social context, and the ethnographer.

Lassiter (1998) explains the relationship between the ethnographer and community members in the following way:

> *Collaborative ethnographers . . . [use] the developing text as a centerpiece for evolving conversation. . . . As the ethnographer reshapes the text to reflect this ongoing process, the text represents only a pause in a larger dialogue. . . . The final published document, then, is seen as in process rather than definitive. . . . [It] produce[s] meaningful understandings of cultural diversity and . . . reveal[s] alternatives to our own ways of being.*
>
> *(p. 11)*

In adopting a collaborative ethnography grounded in praxis, we aim to accomplish two intellectually and morally significant tasks. The first is to learn from insiders, those who have the most to contribute and who stand to reap the greatest benefit from—ideally positively rather than neutrally or negatively—our collaboration. The second is to share our findings with the people we work with, in an effort toward better understanding. Change does not emanate from the ethnographer, but ethnographic work can lead to change. Creating change is the work of agency, which Duranti (1990) defines "as the causal relationship between participants' actions and certain states of affairs or processes" (p. 646). It's also common for ethnographers to give back to the communities with whom they work. This might mean researching and writing grants that would help with a particular project, or contributing in another way that community members would like.

Davies (1990) reminds us that discursive practices are constitutive (pp. 345–346). That is, we produce who we are through our interactions with other people, and they produce us. All of that happens within relations of power. Issues of agency are always involved in those interactions, and sometimes we can refuse the roles that produce us, and other times it's more difficult. Villenas (1996) has written about what can happen when researchers who are from lower-status groups get marginalized in the research process. She has said, "The 'native' ethnographer is potentially both the colonizer in her university cloak, and the colonized, as a member of the very community that made her 'other' in her research" (p. 345). The reality is that collaborating with a community is complex. There are multiple points of view and conflicts that arise, and the ethnographer must navigate through them.

Hymes' SPEAKING Framework

Along with creating the field of the ethnography of communication, Hymes (1974) introduced a framework for gathering and analyzing ethnographic data. Based on the concept that language use, like all aspects of communal behavior, is patterned and governed by norms, the framework focuses on identifying "the situations and uses, the patterns and function, of speaking as an activity in its own right" (Hymes, 1968, p. 101).

Hymes' framework has influenced many scholars, and his work represents a shift in how researchers have approached language—from what people know about language (competence) to what people do with language (performance) to what people know about what to do with language (communicative competence). Hymes' (1974) mnemonic SPEAKING served as a tool to guide the analysis of a speech event in a speech community, with each letter of the word referring to a different aspect of the event.

SPEAKING

Setting   Where and when does the speech event take place? What materials are part of the setting and play a role in the speech event?

Participants   Who are the participants in the speech event? What are their roles?

Ends   What are the participants' goals? What are the purposes and outcomes of the speech event?

Act Sequence   What is the content, form, and order of all of the messages exchanged?

Key   What attitude do the participants demonstrate? What is the atmosphere or spirit of the event?

Instrumentalities   Does the speech event incorporate channels of speech, writing, signed language, facial expression, and/or gesture?

> What codes—language, dialect, style—are used in the speech event? Do participants alternate among the channels and the codes, and, if so, in what patterns?
> Norms   What are the expectations of and guidelines for interacting and for interpreting participant interaction?
> Genre   What are the categories or types of speech acts that make up the speech event? (Hymes 1974)

The power relationships among people are downplayed in this model, and today we would like to adapt Hymes' approach to include and address relations of power and social position. We also want to update the approach by urging researchers to situate themselves in terms of their positionality in the observation. Who are the researchers, and what does their position allow them to see? That's a question that needs to be addressed throughout the study. How else are we updating the ethnography of communication approach? By trying to understand norms as well as resistance to norms, looking at the center as well as the periphery. By encouraging researchers to embed what they write about in a historical context, making it clear that these practices don't happen in a vacuum. And, finally, using social theory to interpret the data.

While Hymes' work on the Ethnography of Communication has been foundational to our understanding of the social uses of language, it leaves us with questions. Hymes assumed that identifying a speech community was easy. Is it? What if people use more than one language or language style, or mix languages? What if people's identities grow and change over time? What if you are on the margins of the community and not at the center?

●●●●●
Communities of Practice

The questions we've asked above are another reason we want to update Hymes' work. Hymes' focus on normative behavior meant that he ended up dismissing everyone on the margins. That is, all sociocultural landscapes have centers and peripheries, and his focus was on the center and on what "legitimate" speakers could do. Postmodern approaches question the construction of the center. That's what Foucault (1980) was talking about when he said that power/knowledge should be a single concept. The folks at the center of a practice have more power, so their reality gets to be the legitimate knowledge. This idea leads us to ask questions about everyone in a group, widening our scope to include people at the center and at the periphery and to look at the ways they interact.

Hymes defined a speech community as a group of people who agree about the norms for using language. One of the problems with the idea of a speech community was that it was conceptualized as static. Speech communities were unchanging. That is something that needs updating. Along with that, we're not convinced that speech communities are as bounded and distinct as Hymes first imagined them. People's speech practices don't obey borders so neatly. We wonder if the bounded notion of a speech community with rigid norms might have been connected to less developed ideas about identities. Today, we see identities as multiple, fluid, and co-constructed within communities of practice. In a given context, one aspect of identity may be foregrounded. In another setting, that same aspect may be backgrounded. The idea of a single speech community that one belongs to, to the exclusion of all others, is no longer a possibility. Therefore, another concept we had to update in the ethnography of communication approach is that of the speech community. Instead of thinking about speech communities, we prefer the idea of **communities of practice.**

Lave and Wenger introduced the concept of communities of practice in 1991. They said we should study groups of people who share social practices—that is, people who are part of a social group and who produce meanings in their local context. Those meanings might involve language, but they might also involve symbols and multiple modalities of expression. Members of a community of practice may move in and out of different communities. Communities of practice are not static: they are fluid. The community of practice idea helps us explore not just language but the social part of our practices as well. Communities of practice are plural, and that resonates with our having multiple identities that change through time. This concept offers us a way to think about structure (the ways in which we are always already placed in particular social and historical contexts) and agency (the ways we make choices and resist and create change).

Learning to Look at a Community of Practice

This six-minute scene from the film adaptation of Truman Capote's *Breakfast at Tiffany's* is a theatrical depiction, not an example of real life: http://www.youtube.com/watch?v=2nnTSePPCVk. But let's suspend disbelief and imagine that it is a scene from real life. There is a LOT for you to observe in this clip. Imagine yourself as a person who was invited to the party shown in the clip by an acquaintance.

Work in small groups. Use the SPEAKING model to discuss and write down what you observe. Remember to postpone any judgment. A caveat: Don't think of genre in terms of film genres. Think of the scene as a real-life party you were invited to, and think about genre as categories of speech that make up the speech events.

Be aware that this clip is from 1961, and there are some racist stereotypes in it. After you have addressed all of the letters of the SPEAKING model, think about the power relationships in this clip as well. Thinking of this now, not as real life, but as part of U.S. film history, what does the depiction of the Asian neighbor, played by Mickey Rooney, tell you about norms in the depiction of racial difference at the time? Were there any historical events in which you could contextualize the depiction of the Asian neighbor?

Now, talk about a party you have attended. Use the SPEAKING model to describe and understand that experience as well as the power relationships existing among the participants.

You may want to return to this clip to practice taking field notes later in this chapter.

● ● ● ● ●
Becoming Reflexive

Data collection is the heart of ethnographic fieldwork. The key to collecting the data that allows you to develop an understanding of how people make sense of their lives in particular social, cultural, and historical contexts is dependent on a number of things:

1. You, the researcher, understanding and reflecting on your positionality (i.e., what it is possible for you to know given your positions of power and access);
2. Postponing judgment (i.e., taking in everything you perceive and "trying it on" before you evaluate it);
3. Being a participant observer in the sociocultural landscape;
4. Interviewing people, both formally and informally (this may include focus groups);
5. Collecting artifacts (i.e., Facebook postings, emails, texts, drawings, photographs, twitter posts, schoolwork . . . virtually anything);
6. Interpreting the voluminous data you have gathered, with an understanding of the agency-structure continuum (i.e., we do and say things that are innovative, both individually and as members of groups, while at the same time everything all of us do is "always already situated in a social, political, and historical moment" (Tedlock and Mannheim, 1995, p. 5);
7. Sharing your analyses, so that readers can consider the implications of your work in other contexts.

● ● ● ● ●
Your Positionality

Think about who you are and where you are right now, in the social, political, cultural, and historical worlds you inhabit (gulp). We know that's a big, almost unanswerably complex question. But, remember, we said "almost".

There is a theory of knowledge—what is knowable and what isn't—underneath our invitation for you to think about your locations in multiple social worlds. Another name for that theory of knowledge is **epistemology**. That is, rather than thinking we can know everything in the world, we would like to consider the idea that there are certain things you can learn about more easily than other people, because of who you are and your positions of power and/or marginalization. So, for example, if you went to a private school, you might be in a powerful position to study the experiences of students in a private school. That is, you might be able to access that context because of your knowledge and connections. Also, knowing how private schools work, even though there are differences, could be an advantage.

Here's another example: Ruth Gomberg-Muñoz worked her way through college and later graduate school by waiting tables and tending bar. It was in these jobs that she met Mexican immigrant men, most of whom worked as busboys. She ended up doing a study about Mexican immigrant networks in Chicago with her friends and co-workers, called *Labor and Legality: An Ethnography of a Mexican Immigrant Network* (2011). Her power position—her positionality—made that work possible.

Why do we call this **positionality** and not just position? Well, position sounds mostly physical (Could you change position? I can't see over your head . . .) or rhetorical (Can you defend your position on states' rights?). But positionality is about those two things and more. It's about power.

In the 1980s the work of French scholars in the postmodern tradition (Michel Foucault and Pierre Bourdieu are two big names here, among others) became available in English. Scholars in the United States, specifically anthropologists, started to rethink their ideas about how they came to know what they thought they knew. Issues of power and positionality entered the picture.

Ethnographers started to look more critically at the relationships they had with the people they worked with, and the conditions under which they did ethnography. They began to understand that power relationships impacted who and what they could observe, as well as how they interpreted what they experienced. They started to ask, rather belatedly, who benefited from the work they produced. Importantly, the people they studied did the same. This was part of the reflexive turn in the social sciences. There have been lots of turns—the social turn, the cultural turn, the linguistic turn, the narrative turn, the performative turn, the spatial turn—and no doubt there will be many more turns taken. A **turn** is a new perspective on how to interpret ethnographic data.

What Are Some of Your Positionalities?

Talk with a partner. Begin by asking about the social categories they inhabit, including things like race, gender identity, class, ethnicity, sexuality, religious practice, ability, national affiliations, and languages spoken. These are springboards for other identity categories. Then ask your partner about their daily activities. Family? Friends? Work? Hobbies? Social groups or political groups they belong to? Make a list of your partner's social categories. Then your partner will do the same with you.

Compare and contrast your lists.

Your positionality is important. It's more than just brainstorming a list of who you know that may also help you figure out where you might do your study, although that's a part of it. More importantly, situating yourself is about rejecting the idea of a universal subject, or a grand narrative of history. It's a way of saying that local worlds matter.

Your positionality is important because it gives your readers an idea about how the knowledge in your study was produced. When you do the ethnography of communication, the knowledge you produce always comes from your interaction with the people you work with. You are not wearing a labcoat and isolating proteins in petri dishes (unless you are studying scientists who do that work, of course). You are working with people in another part of the real world. And you are part of it. You need to continually reflect on your positionality because there are assumptions that all of us have, based on how we understand our own life experiences. It's your job to reflect on and examine your own assumptions throughout this project.

● ● ● ● ●

Postponing Judgment

Think about what it's like to be in a new context where you don't understand what's going on. You're confused about what you're supposed to do. At the same time, you might have judgments about what other people are doing. It's easy to compare a new situation with related experiences you have had and decide that the new ones aren't the same. Or that somehow they aren't as good.

In Chapter 1, we talked about the idea that in some public schools in Sonora, Mexico, when students are called on, the norm is to stand up and state their answers. If you are used to that way of interacting in a classroom, it may seem strange to find yourself in a U.S. classroom where students might remain seated while they shout out their answers to the teacher. Is one approach better than the other? That's hard to say. Does each approach represent the practices of the entire nation? Absolutely not. It makes sense to observe how things are done and ask questions about them, to gather more information, before making a judgment.

Ethnographers approach their work as learners. Assume that you need more information before you make judgments. Don't be surprised if, as you learn about a particular sociocultural landscape, the things that you were upset about or that you had judgments about fade into the background and become less important. On the other hand, you may think you know what's going on because certain practices remind you of ones that you are familiar with. Be aware of that feeling, and be cautious about it. Your own experiences may get in the way of your being able to really see what's happening.

●●●●●

The CULTURES Model

As we noted earlier, Hymes introduced his SPEAKING framework in the form of a mnemonic device to help us remember the components of a speech event. When participating in a given speech event, we demonstrate our knowledge of what to do and say—our communicative competence—by interacting along the social expectations aligned with each of these components. The ethnographer of communication, in turn, seeks to describe and interpret the *what, how,* and *why* of people's participation in a speech event.

Introduction to the CULTURES Model

Our model takes us back to the definitions of culture offered by Duranti, for whom culture is learned knowledge, spread and shared through communicative means and existing within and among us as a system of mediation, practices, and participation. Like Hymes, we use a mnemonic device to present and aid recall of our model. Our framework is CULTURES, offered to you as a process model for doing the ethnography of communication. Judy has been using an earlier version of this model in her teaching and research for many years, most recently in the context of bioethics (Russe and Kaplan-Weinger, 2013). CULTURES provides the steps through which an ethnographer should progress while gathering the data, completing an analysis, and presenting a description and understanding of a community's ways of knowing, being, and doing. The model is iterative to account for the continuous influence of what we observe and of the knowledge we gain as ethnographers.

If the Model Is Iterative, Does It Ever End?

You may be worried about the idea of doing a research project that goes on forever. We have some tips for figuring out when your project is completed. There are a lot of possibilities:

1. Your assignment is due.
2. You see patterns repeating to the point that there are no new insights.
3. The practice you were studying has come to completion.
4. Your funding has run out.

If you're writing a dissertation, you will find it important to maintain ties to the community and people you are now studying. Feminist ethnographers, such as Patti Lather (1991; Lather and Smithies, 1997) and Patricia MacNamara (2009), say it's important to treat the people in your study with respect rather than as objects of study and to build a sincere and honest relationship that you have the intent of maintaining, even if you decide to no longer conduct research in that community.

Many scholars also find it important to develop reciprocal relationships with communities. You may enter a community to research one thing and find that the people of the community want you to help them research something that is important to them (for example, writing a grant to attain educational funding for the community). Out of a sense of ethics and responsibility, as well as the possibility that you will want to return to the community at some later time, it is very important to maintain ties to the community even when your initial project has been completed.

Given the evolving nature of a community—its flexibility in terms of members and their roles and purposes, activity and dormancy, environments, resources, actions, and communicative means—any model that guides data gathering and analysis of its practices must be cyclical to allow for free movement among all steps in the process. That is why our presentation of the CULTURES model appears as a circle. The circle suggests that there is a relationship among all components of the model; they both depend on and flow into one another. The arrows suggest the flow among the components. It is important to recognize that although the cyclical nature of the model can still be seen as linear in its movement from one component to another, the circle is recursive and all of its components interact, suggesting that:

1. the ethnographic process of data collection, analysis, and interpretation is conceivably continuous; and

2. at any point in the process, the ethnographer may 'ride an arrow' past one or more of the components to, for example, compile knowledge, share implications or locate patterns, or engage in further interviewing, participant observation, and artifact collection.

We acknowledge that this diagram makes the ethnography of communication look neat and simple to do. It's not. The only stable parts of this cycle are the beginning and the end. Real life is complicated and messy. Studying people in naturalistic settings is filled with events you can't control and that you don't want to control. The point is that with this model, we offer you a guide for engaging in one of the most exciting and complex kinds of social science research you can imagine. There are things you can learn through ethnographic research that you cannot learn any other way.

●●●●●

Components of the CULTURES Model

In the chapters that follow, each component of the CULTURES model will be further explained, and you will have opportunities to practice ethnographic exercises as you complete your own ethnographic project. What follows is a brief explanation of each component.

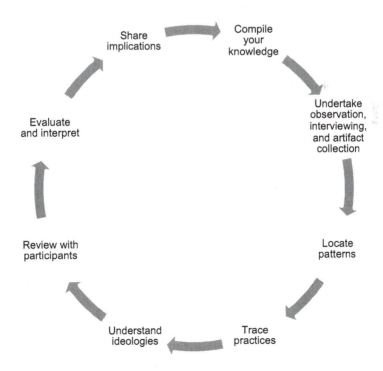

Compile Your Knowledge

As you think about how you will select a community of practice you want to work with, you have to begin by reflecting on your own identities and experiences and thinking about what you would like to explore. For example, Char did a study about how people form their identities and beliefs about the nation in relation to an English language program (DVDs, CDs, and books) called *Inglés sin Barreras*. She had been an English to Speakers of Other Languages (ESOL) teacher with adults and knew lots of students who had bought the program. She had also worked as an editor of ESOL books for adults before she began that project, so her experience in publishing helped her when she talked to the company that produced *Inglés sin Barreras*. You need to think about your own experiences, what interests you, and the project that is "out there", perhaps right in front of your nose. After you have thought about the communities you would like to explore, then you need to think about what you already know about the communities, their members, and their practices. This step asks you to call up your background knowledge or schemata (Piaget, 1929) to help you anticipate what you may encounter. We think of schemata as your having hangers to hang your ideas on. By the way, *schema* is singular, and *schemata* is plural. Athey (2007, p. 50) explains that a schema is "a pattern of repeatable behaviour into which experiences are assimilated and that are gradually co-ordinated." Schemata provide expectations of self and other behavior based on knowledge gained from similar previous behaviors.

Schemata shape what we see as knowledge, as well as what we observe to be important and unimportant in the present moment. They allow us to process, categorize, and understand new information in the context of previously learned knowledge. This is a fundamental process for human cognition, as the vast majority of human behavior is patterned. Storing observed and participated-in behaviors in categories makes a cognitive space in which new behaviors can be sorted. Most often, this process proves beneficial for learning. However, at times the sorting leads to inaccurate categorizing and, therefore, ill-informed and biased interpretations of behaviors and/or those who perform them. If we err in categorizing by assuming that a newly experienced behavior can be interpreted in the same way as a known behavior, we run the risk of imposing an understanding that may not be relevant to any particular way of being. This bias can, in turn, lead to unwarranted generalizations and stereotyping. We must be careful, then, with our application of prior knowledge; however, we don't have much control. What any one of us can best hope for is to be continually cognizant of the role a schema plays in influencing our understanding and behavior. We are reassured in this hope by the fact that our schema is constantly expanding with each new experience.

Undertake Observation, Interviewing, and Artifact Collection

The systematic processes of becoming a participant observer in a community, conducting interviews, and collecting artifacts are the ways you will gain increased understanding of people's experiences at the center and at the periphery of a community of practice. Before going into a community, the ethnographer needs to be concerned with how to identify, locate, and approach a community. This may take time. Conducting interviews, being a participant observer, and collecting artifacts can go on indefinitely. As we mentioned earlier, both internal (you and what you have found out) and external (the end of the semester, changes in the community, funding) variables all impact when you stop collecting data.

Locate Patterns

Equipped with field notes from your participant observation, transcripts of your interviews, and your artifacts (the real thing or photographs), you will now look for patterns in your data. A pattern may be a physical behavior or a statement repeated over time by one participant or a variety of participants. It may also be a theme that arises again and again in the content of what people say. If you see a language practice or a theme repeatedly, it's a pattern. However, there may be exceptions to that pattern. That doesn't mean that you have done something wrong. That's just the messiness of human behavior. You may see patterns that apply to people who are at the center of the community and other patterns that apply to those at the periphery. We always see things that don't fit the pattern. That's OK. The environment in which language practices and behaviors occur and the intent underlying their presence may vary. And that variation may be a pattern. As we explained earlier, these patterns exist because humans behave overwhelmingly systematically and predictably, even though it might not seem like it. Once you have done the ethnography of communication, you will see patterned behavior everywhere (like that greenish color Char couldn't stop noticing). While patterns emerge organically in human behavior and necessarily, then, in ethnographic data, they are the foundation of our coming to understand what's going on in a community of practice. Later, you will look at the patterns in your data and interpret those patterns in relation to social theory.

Trace Practices

The practices we engage in every day are patterned. As human beings, we regulate our behavior because we are wired for systems and expectations. Wherever recurrent behavior is identified in field notes, responses, or documents, there are underlying systems calling for and guiding that behavior.

Understand Ideologies

Digging deeper into data analysis, we need to consider ideologies. Ideologies are values and beliefs about the world that guide people's behavior. At the same time, within a given community, there will be ideological diversity. Not everyone will think the same way. These ideologies are beliefs about why the world is organized as it is and how people think it should be organized. These beliefs may relate to particular ways of using language (for example, standard varieties versus alternate varieties) or to the use of specific languages (for example, Spanish versus English) in given environments and the ideologies associated with them. While behaviors, what we do or what we say, may differ among and within various communities, we often find great similarities in values and ideologies across these same communities.

Review With Participants

One way ethnographers of communication ensure the trustworthiness of their work is through member checks—confirming or disconfirming their understanding of what they have seen and heard. The participants in your study will help you to make sure you understood them correctly. Oftentimes, there are contradictions between formal interviews and data gathered through participant observation and/or analysis of documents or artifacts.

For example, what one sees in the day-to-day running of a non-profit organization (participant observation) may be in contrast with what the mission statement says (document collection) and with what the director of the organization says (interview). All data collection methods answer some questions but at the same time leave many questions unanswered. Because ethnographic research is recursive, new questions continually emerge. We gather data through participant observation, interviewing, and artifact collection. Then we turn that data into field notes, transcriptions, and descriptions of artifacts. Once we identify patterns or themes in the data, we move to finding the right theories to help us understand it. Member checks may happen once you have interpreted your data as well. But it's always important to check your understanding.

Evaluate and Interpret

Your ethnographic analysis has importance beyond the fulfillment of a class assignment. Sharing your work with a larger audience makes it useful and meaningful to the community you worked with and others, as well as to larger scholarly communities. This is the time when you let your data speak to you and tell you what kind of theoretical works you might use to interpret what's going on. Notice that we didn't start by saying, "Choose a theorist and then find data to support those theories." It's exactly the other way around with the ethnography of communication. Rather than starting with a theory you want to prove or disprove, ethnography is inductive research. You collect your data, and then you figure out what it means. You let the data lead you, not the other way around.

Share Implications

You might say, "But I just learned about one context . . . how can it matter to other people?" You study a particular context or community, interpret what is going on, and then other people, people attending scholarly conferences and people reading scholarly journals, will find implications in what you found for their own contexts. We strongly encourage you to also share what you found in a presentation to the people in the community you studied. To do this well, you need to really think about who your audience is and how best to communicate with them.

There are different ways that you can present your research to a scholarly community. And there are still other ways to share your findings with the community and with your friends and others who are interested in what they can learn from your experience. Ethnographers need to get feedback on their work through presentations (in the classroom and/or at conferences). Writing up and sharing your work is a crucial way for you to review and synthesize the knowledge you have produced. On the scholarly, community, and personal levels, your work will result in growth.

Now that you have an overview of the research process of the ethnography of communication, you have to spend some time thinking about what you will be exploring and how you will conduct your research. Talk with your classmates and your instructor about your ideas. Your first step in the research process is to write an Institutional Review Board (IRB) proposal. Once your proposal is approved, then, and only then, can you start your research.

●●●●●
The IRB Process

Before you begin your ethnography of communication study, you need to write an Institutional Review Board (IRB) proposal. This will help you think about the specifics of what you want to find out and how you will do it. Actually, everyone who does research with human beings has to write an IRB proposal and get it approved before they begin. It's federal law. We have IRBs because there have been terrible abuses committed by scientists in the name of research. During the Holocaust, Nazi doctors performed horrific experiments on concentration camp prisoners. To learn more about these atrocities, go to the website of the Holocaust Memorial Museum, at http://www. ushmm.org/wlc/en/article.php?ModuleId=10005168 . But that isn't all. In the United States, the Tuskegee Experiments went on from 1932 to 1972. African American men who were poor and lived in rural areas were studied to see what the long-term impact of syphilis was on the body. They were told they were getting treatment, which existed at the time, but they weren't. They died painful deaths, and their families were infected. It was an atrocity as well. To learn more about the Tuskegee Experiments, we encourage you to watch the excellent film *Miss Evers' Boys*.

The first step on the road to the IRB proposal is to take the CITI training, which is comprised of two online tests. CITI stands for Collaborative Institutional Training Initiative, and you can find it at https://www.citiprogram.org/members/index.cfm?pageID=50. You need to create a profile, and then you need to take the following tests:

1. Social and Behavioral Researchers (Faculty & Students)
2. Social and Behavioral Responsible Conduct of Research

You will get an electronic certificate that shows you have passed these tests. Save it, as you will need to submit it to the IRB with your proposal. The website www.irbnet.org funnels proposals to the correct review boards and has templates to help with proposal writing. Both Char's and Judy's universities use this system, as do most colleges and universities throughout the country. Non-profit organizations and government agencies also use this system. You will need to register on www.irbnet.org and create a project. Download all the forms and templates, and use them to craft your proposal. It's detail-oriented work, but it doesn't take too long. Since you are doing an ethnography of communication study, it's likely that you can't know all of the questions you want to ask beforehand. That's OK. You can explain in your proposal that while you have some preliminary questions (which you will include), ethnographic studies involve discovery through long-term involvement in a community of practice. That means more questions will emerge in the process of conducting the study. You just have to explain that, and you'll be fine. Remember, the people on the review board are busy professors who are reading proposals as a service to their universities. They will be from a variety of disciplines, so you need to make your proposal understandable to a general audience.

You might be wondering why you have to take these tests and write an IRB proposal if you won't be doing medical research. Ethnographic research can't hurt people, right? Well, wrong. There have been abuses among social scientists as well. Back in the 1960s, sociologist Laud Humphreys wrote about men who had sex with other men in public restrooms. He used deception in his study. And psychologist Stanley Milgram conducted a study about obedience to authority that caused great emotional stress for participants. We have learned things about social science research since the 1960s. People need to know what they're getting involved in, and they need to know what the risks and benefits of the study will be for them.

While it's possible to do a small study that is a course requirement without getting IRB approval, you will never be allowed to publish the results of that work. What if you uncover something important? It would be a shame for you to not be able to publish your work. For that reason, we encourage you to get IRB approval for your study. Depending on your college or university, and the kind of study you envision, it can be a process that takes only a couple of weeks.

As you think about the group with whom you are going to do your study, you should know that there are some groups who are special populations in the eyes of IRB members. That means they need to be protected more than other people because their ability to consent to being in a study may be compromised by their situation. They are children under 18, elderly people, people in prison, undocumented people, and people with cognitive disabilities. It's not that you can't do studies with them—it's just that your study will go under special review, and it may take longer for the IRB committee to approve your study. Also, if you are doing a study at a school, for example, your proposal will need to be approved by the school district's IRB. The same is true for doing a study at a prison. If you want to do a study with Native American people, your proposal must go through the tribal council. You need to consciously build relationships not only with the people you are going to work with but with the institutions that will evaluate your study as well. After you have submitted your IRB proposal to your university, it is likely that you will have to do a few revisions. Don't feel as though you've failed. It's common to have revisions. You will be given a period of time to make those changes, you will submit them, and your study will be approved. Once your IRB proposal is approved, you can begin to conduct your ethnography of communication study.

Talking Together

Take a moment to read about confidentiality and privacy as described on www.irbnet.org, under "Consent Forms". What might the issues of confidentiality and privacy be in the following settings?

1. A corporate office
2. A person's home
3. A public school classroom
4. A place of worship
5. A hospital
6. A non-profit organization
7. An Indian Reservation

● ● ● ● ●

Wrapping Up

With guidance about writing your IRB proposal and the CULTURES model in hand, you are ready to consider the community in which you will undertake your fieldwork. The chapters that follow will take you through the CULTURES model in a step-by-step way. We wish you a great start!

This article and others that appear in various chapters as examples of ethnographic inquiry can be accessed through your university library, and the information you need to search for them is available in the References section at the end of this chapter:

● ● ● ● ●

References

Athey, C. (2007). *Extending thought in young children: A parent-teacher partnership.* London: Paul Chapman.

Davies, B. (1990). Agency as a form of discursive practice: A classroom scene observed. *British Journal of Sociology of Education, 11*(3), 341–361. Retrieved from http://www.jstor.org/stable/1392847

Duranti, A. (1990). Politics and grammar: Agency in Samoan political discourse. *American Ethnologist, 17*(4), 646–666. Retrieved from http://www.jstor.org/stable/645706

Edwards, B. (Director). (1961). Breakfast at Tiffany's [Motion Picture]. United States: Paramount.

Foucault, M. (1980). *Power/knowledge: Selected interviews and other writings, 1972–1977.* C. Gordon (Ed.). New York: Pantheon.

Freire, P. (2006). *Pedagogy of the oppressed*. New York: Continuum.

Genzuk, M. (2003). A synthesis of ethnographic research. Occasional Papers Series. Los Angeles, CA: Center for Multilingual, Multicultural Research, Rossier School of Education. Retrieved from http://www.bcf.usc.edu/~genzuk/Ethnographic_Research.pdf

Gomberg-Munoz, R. (2011). *Labor and legality: An ethnography of a Mexican immigrant network.*

Hymes, D. 1974. Foundations in sociolinguistics: An ethnographic approach. Philadelphia: University of Pennsylvania Press.

Labov, W. 1972. *Sociolinguistic patterns*. Philadelphia: University of Pennsylvania Press.

Lassiter, L. E. (1998). *The power of Kiowa song: A collaborative ethnography.* Tucson: University of Arizona Press.

Lassiter, L. E. (2005). *The Chicago guide to collaborative ethnography.* Chicago: University of Chicago Press.

Lather, P.A. (1991). Getting smart: Feminist research and pedagogy with/in the postmodern. New York: Routledge.

Lather, P.A., & Smithies, C. S. (1997). *Troubling the angels: Women living with HIV/AIDS.* Boulder, CO: Westview.

Lave, J., & Wenger, E. (1991). *Situated learning: Legitimate peripheral participation.* Cambridge: Cambridge University Press.

Macnamara, P. (2009). Feminist ethnography: Storytelling that makes a difference. *Qualitative Social Work June, 8* 161–177.

Piaget, J. (1929). *The child's conception of the world.* Lanham, MD: Rowman and Littlefield.

Russe, S., & Kaplan-Weinger, J. (2013, March 16–19). *Language, CULTURE, and bioethics: Using narrative methods to update the patient-provider connection.* Annual meeting of the American Association of Applied Linguistics, Dallas, TX.

Tedlock, D., & Mannheim, B. (1995). *The dialogic emergence of culture.* Urbana: University of Illinois Press.

Villenas, S. (1996). The colonizer/colonized Chicana ethnographer: Identity, marginalization, and co-optation in the field. *Harvard Educational Review, 66*(4), 711–731.

5
•••••
Compile Your Knowledge

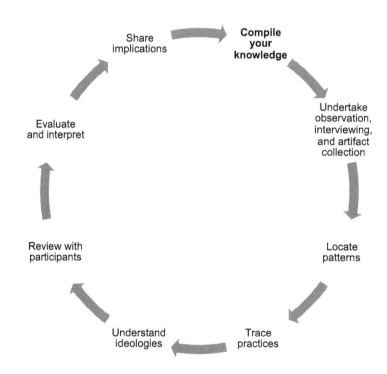

So what do we mean when we talk about knowledge? We would like you to consider the idea that facts that everyone agrees with aren't just floating around out there in the world for you to reach up and grab onto. Historically, scholars began to think about the social world as parallel to the physical world. That is, if gravity works the same way in the Punjab as it does in Antarctica, then social "facts" must be the same. But scholars have learned that is simply not the case. Social and cultural knowledge is particular. It's specific to its context. With your ethnography of communication research, you will produce knowledge, and what you produce will be related to your positionality. That is, your lenses on the world, what you can see and understand, have something to do with your history, your experiences, and your expectations. All of these things influence your perceptions and, therefore, what you see as important in the context in which you are doing research. Think about what you can see when you look through the lens of a camera. The frame includes certain things but leaves many things out, right? Each of us has lenses through which we see and understand the world. But no one has all the possible lenses.

Thinking Together

Complete each sentence below with one word (it's OK to put *a/an* in front of that one word). After you have completed your 20 attributes, show your list to a classmate. Look at your partner's list. How might these attributes impact your partner's positionality? Might there be privilege that your partner is unaware of? Is there marginality that may impact your partner's positionality?

Who am I?

1. I am . . .
2. I am . . .
3. I am . . .
4. I am . . .
5. I am . . .
6. I am . . .
7. I am . . .
8. I am . . .
9. I am . . .
10. I am . . .
11. I am . . .
12. I am . . .
13. I am . . .
14. I am . . .
15. I am . . .
16. I am . . .
17. I am . . .
18. I am . . .
19. I am . . .
20. I am . . .

This activity is adapted from the work of Halasz and Kaufman (2008).

We hope this exercise helps you to think about how your own lenses for seeing the world are produced. Remember, in the ethnography of communication, you are the instrument through which data is collected, analyzed, and interpreted. It's vital that you practice becoming aware of your own positionality. And practice is a key part of that sentence, because reflecting on your beliefs isn't something you do once, at the beginning of your study, and then never do again. It's an iterative process that you engage in throughout your study.

So, again, what is knowledge? And how do you get it? And perhaps an even more difficult question to answer: What do you *do* with it?

When Judy was completing her graduate work at Georgetown University, one of her professors, Deborah Tannen, shared a film with her class that made them think about knowledge and how it is produced. *The Pear Film*, as it has come to be called, was put together by linguist Wallace Chafe (n.d.).

Interpreting Together

Here's a link to that movie: http://www.youtube.com/watch?v=bRNSTxTpG7U
Watch the film. On a piece of paper or on a computer, write what you saw.
Read aloud what you wrote. Listen to your classmates' versions of what they saw.
How is their version like yours? How does their version differ from yours? What do you think accounts for those similarities and differences?

●●●●●

Knowledge and Human Behavior

Human behavior is patterned. Overwhelmingly so. We participate in daily life and interact with one another in ways we have done before. Back in the 1850s, Marx reminded us that "Men [*sic*] make their own history, but they do not make it as they please; they do not make it under self-selected circumstances, but under circumstances already given and transmitted from the past" (Marx, 1963, p. 15). That is, all of us are doing what we are doing right now within the flow of history. It may feel as though we have invented our behavior, and sometimes we have, but none of us is outside the social world. There is no outside of the social world.

Our patterns help us create knowledge structures or 'schema' (Bartlett, 1932). Schema allow us to have a context for interpreting other people's behavior based on what we have learned from similar contexts. Imagine if we experienced everything in our lives as a new, unique experience. Just meeting someone new would be a huge task. We wouldn't have any categories to help us understand that new being, so we wouldn't know things we take for granted now. Is this being a person? Does the being have language? If so, what language is it? Should you greet the being? If so, how? So many questions.

Life is a process of calling on existing knowledge or schema in order to be able to anticipate what will come next. As humans, we need to be able to do this. Our minds work as categorizing instruments sorting new experiences into categories of knowledge—some pre-existing, some newly formed, some hybrids of new and old. These are categories that we draw on to have successful social interactions. For Bartlett (1932), "whenever there is any order or regularity of behaviour, a particular response is possible only because it is related to other similar responses which have been serially organised, yet which operate, not simply as individual members coming one after another, but as a unitary mass" (p. 3). That is, we are constantly creating a repository of knowledge, which we categorize and recategorize all the time. That knowledge is part of a living, breathing whole. And that knowledge is dynamic, and is co-constructed again and again in our communities of practice.

Working Together

Your instructor will divide the class into an even number of small groups or two large groups. The instructions for each group are in the boxes below. After each group completes its' work, the whole group will come together to compare and contrast ideas.

Group 1

Your job is to come up with a list of the kinds of cars you think the people listed below would drive.

Note the year and condition you think the car would be in.

Person	Car
NBA player	
WNBA player	
Single mother of three with a high school degree	
University president	
Construction worker	
Adult education ESOL teacher	
Civil engineer	
Middle-school principal	
Postal worker	
Retired couple	
Gang member	
Hairstylist	

1. Why did you match certain cars and people?
2. What stereotypes were you employing?
3. Do you have any unexamined stereotypes?
4. Are cars accurate markers of social class? Political perspective?

Do you have a car? If so, what does it say about you? If you don't have a car, is there a car you would like to own? What would that car say about your location in the social hierarchy?

Group 2

Your job is to come up with a list of the kind of people you think would drive these cars.

Give some descriptive information about the person you think would drive each car.

Car	Person
Honda Civic	
Hummer	
Audi S4	
Saturn L Series	
Ford pickup truck	
Dodge Caravan	
Lincoln Towncar	
Ford Festiva	
Kia Sorento SUV	
Hyundai Accent	
Toyota Prius	
Subaru Outback	

1. Why did you match certain cars and people?
2. What stereotypes were you employing?
3. Do you have any unexamined stereotypes?
4. Are cars accurate markers of social class? Political perspective?

Do you have a car? If so, what does it say about you? If you don't have a car, is there a car you would like to own? What would that car say about your location in the social hierarchy?

*This activity was adapted from the work of Tiemann, Davis, and Eide (2006).

● ● ● ● ●

Ethnographic Knowledge

What is ethnographic knowledge? It's the knowledge that comes from understanding what a group of people know and the structured meanings they create. It typically focuses on problems or questions that are basic to social and cultural life. There is a Mexican immigrant community in Tucson, Arizona, whose members live in a neighborhood where the water was contaminated by the local airport. Children started dying of rare forms of cancer, and many people in the community got sick. In spite of the fact that most people in the community were undocumented and did not speak English, they organized and won a class-action suit against the company that poisoned their water. How did that process happen? That's a question that can be answered through ethnographic research. Ethnographic research is exceptionally good for understanding processes.

The idea of ethnographic research is to go deeply into a particular context, and to generalize within that context, not to generalize across contexts, as is done in quantitative approaches. Ethnographers think about how to make their findings trustworthy (Maxwell, 2010). And ethnographic research isn't always about difference. Sometimes it's about similarities.

Because of the human need to categorize in order to comprehend— to understand the new through the old, to match new knowledge with existing knowledge—when we have decided on a community to research, we will naturally begin calling on our entire schema, including our schema of that community. Even if we know nothing beyond where to find members of that community, or what languages they speak, we will pull from what we know to start developing a connection. What we hear as we talk to the participants in our study immediately gets processed and understood in the context of what we already know. This is something our brains do so that we are not overloaded with information we cannot process. However, it is also a potentially perilous practice because it may lead to ethnocentric interpretations based not on what we come to observe in a community but on what we think we already know about a community. This is the irony; our schema exists so we can depend on it for guidance in new situations. Yet if we do not reflect on our stereotypes and where they come from, we will see only what exists in our schema. We may have a difficult time making sense of a situation and be closed to what we have not previously observed. We may find ourselves ignoring important information in order to save ourselves from having to process something for which we don't have a schema. Think back to what you and your classmates wrote about *The Pear Film*. How does what you just read about schema and ethnographic knowledge explain the similarities and differences in what you wrote earlier?

●●●●●

Rich Points

Anthropologist Michael Agar (1996) writes about **'rich points'**—actions or features of a community that "crop up on the surface and signal the vast wealth below" (p. 108). Agar explains that when we enter a social situation that is unfamiliar, we take note of these rich points because we don't expect them. They strike us as unusual because, as Agar explains, we lack the communicative competence to interact within and understand the community in which they normally occur. Rich points help us learn more, in spite of our schemata. We take advantage of rich points as our entry into a social world. We wonder, for example, when that action occurs and who can perform it; when that feature shows up, must it be presented in a particular way? And, ultimately, what meanings does that behavior have for members of that community?

One of Judy's favorite rich points is a phrase she heard at a Sunday morning service at a church associated with the Christian Pentecostal Assembly of God in a Chicago suburb. After the service ended, Judy was standing in the hallway outside the worship hall. Nearby were two women speaking to each other. Not one to eavesdrop, Judy did not note the content of their conversation, but she did take note of the way they said 'goodbye' to each other. That leave-taking stood out for its unusual words. Following Agar, we might say that the rest of the conversation, spoken at the same level of loudness as the leave-taking, did not stand out because its content matched Judy's expectations—even though she was not actively listening to it. The last utterance, though, was new. Judy remembers hearing one of the women as she walked away utter some form of a 'goodbye' before the other woman responded, 'Yes. Here, there, and in the air.'

Judy's casual standing by at a polite distance immediately turned into focused attention, at that same polite distance. Now, however, Judy wanted to hear the next utterance. Certainly what was said next would provide some clue to what that utterance meant. However, there was no further talk between these women. Their conversation had ended. What could that utterance have meant?

If Judy had been a member of the community and had had the communicative competence of its members, this utterance would not have drawn her attention. In other words, if she were a member of the community, it would not have been a rich point. But it was, and it drew Judy into the community and led her to ask more questions.

Luckily, Judy had someone she could ask—the friend who was a member of the congregation. She served, in this situation, as Judy's **key participant**—a participant who explains things to the researcher and who is a savvy communicator across cultural contexts. Judy found the friend who had invited her to the service and told her what she had seen and heard. With the context of a leave-taking as the action, and of the Assembly of God church as the setting, her friend was able to mine her own communicative competence for the answer to Judy's question. 'Here, there, and in the air', uttered where, when, and by whom it was uttered, refers to the rapture—humans' rising to Heaven with Christ as life on Earth comes to its end. This is an interpretation of 1 Thessalonians 5:16–18, which is followed by many Pentecostal Christians. In the context of the time this utterance was made (following the Sunday morning service), who made it (one woman responding to another as they were parting from each other), and the religious ideology of the speaker (and one can assume the hearer if one assumes the speaker believed she would be understood), this utterance counts as an expression not only of leave-taking but also of faith in the life, death, and resurrection of Jesus Christ and his followers.

A second example is also tied to a religious community. Judy has noticed another leave-taking behavior among students who are Muslim. At the end of class, as students are packing up their notebooks and textbooks, we wish our students a good day or weekend and often follow that with 'See you next class.' The non-Islamic students reply with 'You too!', or 'OK, see you', or 'Bye'. However, many of the Islamic students respond with the Arabic 'insha' Allah', an utterance that marks the speaker's recognition that his or her return to class is up to Allah— literally, 'the God' in Arabic. This ideology is not unique to Muslims and, in fact, shows up in the phrase 'God willing' in the English usage of American Jews and 'If it be God's will' in the speech of some Christians. It's common to hear the response to "adios" (goodbye) in many Latin American countries as "Si Dios quiere" (if God wills it). While there are differences across cultural contexts, there are also similarities.

The way language is used in these two situations shows what Laura Ahearn (2012) calls the "socially charged life of language", the relationship between language use and ideologies. Ahearn draws this idea from the work of Bakhtin (1981), who said, speaking of language, that "each word tastes of the context and contexts in which it has lived its socially charged life . . ." (p. 293). In ethnography of communication, we think about the relationship between language, culture, and thought. There are debates about how deeply one aspect influences the others. Some people believe language strongly influences thought; others believe the connection is a weak one. Still others are somewhere in between. We see language, culture, and thought as inexorably intertwined and "mutually influencing" (Ahearn, 2012, p. 95).

● ● ● ● ●

Culture

> **Talking Together**
>
> Talk with a partner. What do you think of when you hear the word *culture*?
> Can you give examples of culture from your own experiences?

Now, here is a definition from Duranti (1997), who sees culture as:

a. Distinct from nature
b. Knowledge
c. Communication
d. A system of mediation
e. A system of practices
f. A system of participation

So we learn culture(s), and that knowledge includes how to inter-act and understand other people within a community. It also includes daily practices in which beliefs about the world are embedded. As it is learned, cultural knowledge is shared with, or communicated to, others within and outside of a community. Culture is the mediator or means for informing others and becoming informed of the practices one needs to engage in to be a communicatively competent participant within a community. And, finally, culture plus language is the means for solidifying community membership in the sharing of knowledge.

> **Talking Together**
>
> Talk to the partner you worked with before.
>   Compare your definitions to Duranti's. Are they similar? Different? In what ways?

Sometimes cultural knowledge is something we are unaware of. This is especially true for people from dominant social groups. People whose cultural knowledge is not part of the mainstream are usually made aware of the "outsiderness" of their knowledge through formal schooling. Laundra and Sutton (2006) updated Adrian Dove's "Chit-ling Test of Intelligence" to demonstrate the cultural and linguistic knowledge bias of standardized tests. Here are a few examples of the questions from their test (p. 375):

1. Translate this phrase: "Jet to the jects."
   a. Run home.
   b. Walk to the store.
   c. Walk to the home of your significant other.
   d. Go to the projects.
2. What is the most popular dance that is done at almost every Black family function?
   a. The Hustle
   b. The Electric Slide
   c. Stepping
   d. The Bump

Answers: 1 (d); 2 (b).

How did you do? It depends on who you spend time with, doesn't it? Knowledge is also connected to power relations. Foucault thought knowledge/power should be one concept, because they were so inseparable. Really knowing the answers to these two questions comes from experience in a community (being a good guesser doesn't count). What kind of knowledge do we have as members of a community or cultural group? Cultural knowledge exists on at least two levels—one is an active or **explicit level**, and the other is a passive or **tacit level**. Typically, tacit knowledge is acquired through living and participating in a community. All that you observe gets taken in and stored and, when needed, gets called on or activated so you know what to do and say. When you are from a marginalized group, you often have to learn how to exist in multiple worlds, by having explicit and tacit knowledge about your own group and about the dominant group or groups. Initially, it was what W.E.B. DuBois (1994) called "double consciousness". Perhaps today it's more multiplicitous. Implicit knowledge is the kind of thing you "just know". It's only when someone asks you to explain it that you have the opportunity to make it explicit.

Reflecting Together

How do you know where to sit in a classroom?

Do you think about where to sit each time you enter a classroom? If not, how do you know where to sit?

Do you sit in the same place in each classroom, if that seat is available? If so, why?

Do you sit with people you know? People you don't know? What do you do if you don't know anyone in the class?

Do you consider how far from or close to the teacher you need to be so you can see or hear well?

Do you not think about where to sit at all but just wind up in any empty seat?

It's interesting to think about why we make the choices we make when we are going to be with others. When those choices are consciously made or even made without thought, they end up saying something about who we are. Where we sit, who we sit with, what we wear—those are all symbols of our identity. Let's try another situation. Who did you greet today when you came into class? Did you say 'hi' to classmates or to your teacher? If so, what did you actually say? Did you use their names when you greeted them? If so, which name did you choose? Their first name? Their last name? Did you greet your teacher? Did you use your teacher's first name, last name, or a title like Dr. or Professor? How much thought did you give it before deciding? The way we address others—our address-form usage—is norm governed, and we typically don't think about it too much. However, if you are from a cultural/linguistic context where the forms of address for professors or people in authority are more formal than those typically used in the United States, you may make a point of using a more respectful way of speaking than it seems to you your classmates do. That might make your language use more explicit. Although that usage may put you outside the common practices of language use among the dominant group, your choice of using that language may feel truer to yourself.

Think about your language practices now. Why did you use the forms of address that you chose with your teacher and classmates? There could be many reasons for your choices. You may have used your classmates' first names because they are close to you in age. You may have used your teacher's title (Professor, Dr.) because some quality or characteristic makes you different from your teacher. Address forms are part of social interaction. We make our choices from all the address forms available to us based on the communicative competence we in our multiple communities. Norms are not the only practices in a group. Ethnographers of communication can observe these usages to understand both the center and the periphery of a community.

●●●●●

Looking at Practices and Norms

Those who share membership in a given community of practice are guided in their actions by the knowledge they share. But that doesn't mean that everyone acts, thinks, and talks in the same way. Rather, it means members have an idea (communicative competence) of how things are supposed to be, regardless of what they really do. And that communicative competence isn't just about what you say. It's common for us to talk about the multiple modalities people use to communicate. Of course, speaking and writing come to mind first. But other modalities include space, sound, and gestures (Kalantzis and Cope, 2012). For example, members of the same community of practice will likely use and expect others in their community to address them the same way. Referring back to Lave and Wenger (1991), we see this knowledge as emanating through interaction, acquired tacitly or explicitly through exposure to and interaction with others. Practices can be understood as our socially influenced norm-governed actions, as well as those that defy norms. They are governed by things we "just know", most of the time. So our multimodal expressions (speaking, writing, the ways we use space, sound, and gesture) are shaped by the communities we belong to and their norms. However, norms are just one part of a community. Communities always have centers and peripheries. They are not homogeneous, even though they may share many practices and ideologies. Earlier forms of the ethnography of communication focused only on norms and ignored all other behavior. We see the ethnography of communication as an approach that is robust enough to look at all of the practices within a community—practices of people at the center (the norm), people at the periphery (the outliers), and the people in between.

●●●●●
Looking at Ideologies

The term *ideology* has a long and complicated history, from French Enlightenment thinkers who used it to promote the application of the scientific method, to Marx's use of the term to mean false consciousness, or a misunderstanding of how the world really works. We think about ideologies as political, social, and cultural beliefs people have about the world and their own practices, as well as the practices of other people. Values are ideologies as well. For example, we all have language ideologies, or beliefs about the right ways to speak. Our language ideologies may include notions about the appropriateness of mixing languages such as Spanish and English in a particular context, or about the sacredness of a language such as Hebrew or Navajo. We also have ideologies about different kinds of people and about the ways the world works. Ideologies are political as well as personal. Ideological practices pervade our communication. Ideologies are often unconscious, and as ethnographers of communication, one of our goals is to uncover the ideologies that undergird our daily practices.

Thinking Together

Watch the 10-minute video *Undocubus Puganini Po'kwin*, made by Native American youth who are part of the YouthCineMedia project (YouthCineMedia 2013). You can find the video at http://www.youtube.com/watch?v=TihR4 NyExJ8. The motto of the YouthCineMedia project is "creating change through the eyes of today's youth". This is an expressly political video. Listen for ideologies (beliefs about the world), and make a list of them. Sometimes it's easier to notice political ideologies when they are explicit, as some of these are. But others are more implicit.

After you have made your list of the ideologies you heard, get into small groups and discuss them. Are there any that were implicit? What were they?

●●●●●
What Is a Pattern?

In the exercise above, you identified ideologies that presented themselves in patterned ways. Every day, we choose from repertoires of linguistic and multimodal practices when we interact, but what we choose is not entirely by chance. That is, we make choices within the boundaries of certain expectations. Expectations we have about our own and others' practices exist because of the norms we follow or don't follow. The fact that our practices are to some degree limited means we attend—usually unconsciously—to the norms of our communities. For example, where Char lives, along the U.S.–Mexico border, it's common for people to hug each other and give an "air kiss" on one cheek to say hello and goodbye. This is a more traditionally Mexican form of greeting that is common on the U.S. side of the border, and Char has adopted the practice (although she didn't grow up with it). But Char has noticed a pattern in her own greeting practice. When she interacts one-on-one with White people who she knows are from other places, she doesn't greet them the way she greets everyone else. She is likely to look them in the eye and say hello. That's the way she learned to greet people in the Midwest. So saying hello and goodbye with the "air kiss" and a hug is a pattern. But looking people in the eye and saying hello is also a pattern.

When we identify patterns, we look at the repetitive nature and the social context of those everyday practices. Context matters.

●●●●●
What Is a Practice?

Practices are all of the things we do, say, write, and believe. By looking at our social practices, we come to see that human beings are ruled by structures and, at the same time, are individuals. In the discipline of psychology, the world is often seen to be comprised of individual actors who are free to do what they choose. In the social sciences, the world is often seen as determined by social structures that constrict the possibilities of individuals. Practice theory comes from the work of Bourdieu (1977) and is a way of bridging the gap between the larger social structures in which we live and our everyday actions. When we look at social practices, we see a world of both structure and agency. We are neither dire determinists nor individualist optimists. Through the lens of practice theory, it is possible for our daily practices to be both structured and creative.

● ● ● ● ●

Ideologies, Practices, and Patterns

We can also use a metaphor to visualize the relationship between ideologies, practices, and patterns. Edward T. Hall (1976) is credited with the iceberg metaphor to distinguish the explicit from tacit aspects of culture and of cultural knowledge. The iceberg also helps us think about the role ideologies play in constructing our daily practices. An iceberg lies both above and below the waterline. Estimates are that only one-eighth of an iceberg can be seen above the water. With respect to this metaphor, we can say our daily practices are the part we can see above the water. The ideologies that shape our quotidian practices are hard to see. Stuart Hall (1996) says that the ideologies beneath a conversation, an utterance, or a text are rarely visible at first glance. You can't see a person as the tip of the iceberg and say, "Because you look the way you do, I know what the ideologies below you are." That is, we don't believe certain ideas because of one aspect of our identities, such as race. We are more than just our social locations, even when we bring them all together. Hall suggests that we are always looking for ideologies that lie beneath the surface and that they are complex, often mystifying, and always in flux.

We follow the cultural or community practices that are laid down for us—explicitly or tacitly—but we also have creative ideas. We are both structured and structuring, all the time. Out of our ideologies arise our actual observable practices. You can take a look at a number of representations of the iceberg model of culture online. Just do a Google search "of the iceberg model of culture" and see how the relationship between practices, ideologies, and patterns has been represented using this analogy.

To help us understand how the iceberg image clarifies the connection between practices, ideologies, and their patterns, let's return to our rich point about leave-taking—Arabic-speaking students who say, "insha Allah" and Spanish speakers who say, "Si Dios quiere". Both phrases mean that returning to class is "in God's hands". That is, they have an ideology, a belief that returning to class isn't solely their decision. Attending class will not be in their hands, but in G-d's hands. There's another practice, Judy, as a person of the Jewish faith, writes the word 'God' with a dash for the 'o'. The name of God is holy, and anything it is written upon is holy as well. Therefore, because paper can be crumpled up, torn, and thrown away, to avoid abusing the name of G-d, some Jews do not write the name in full.

Are "insha' Allah" and "Si Dios quiere" simply ways of saying goodbye? We can think of these phrases as utterances that sit on icebergs. They remind us that life is uncertain and that many things are outside our control. So the language **patterns** are "Insha Allah" and "Si Dios quiere". The **practices** in which these patterns are embedded are leave-taking routines that recognize and share verbally that one's hopes or future plans are up to G-d. The **ideologies** are that Allah or G-d, and not people, is responsible for every moment of the future, including our hopes and dreams. Clues about our ideologies, our beliefs about the world, are everywhere. We just need to look.

This article and others that appear in various chapters as examples of ethnographic inquiry can be accessed through your university library, and the information you need to search for them is available in the References section at the end of this chapter:

●●●●●
_____

References

Agar, M. (1996). *Language shock: Understanding the culture of conversation.* New York: Morrow.

Ahearn, L. (2012). *Living language: An introduction to linguistic anthropology.* New York: Wiley-Blackwell.

Bakhtin, M. M. (1981). *The dialogic imagination: Four essays.* M. Holquist (Ed. and Trans.). Austin: University of Texas Press.

Bartlett, F. C. (1932). *Remembering: A study in experimental and social psychology.* Cambridge: Cambridge University Press. Retrieved from http://www.bartlett.psychol.cam.ac.uk/TheoryOfRemembering.htm

Bourdieu, P. (1977). *An outline of a theory of practice.* Cambridge: Oxford University Press.

Chafe, W. (n.d.). The Pear Film. Retrieved from http://www.youtube.com/watch?v=bRNSTxTpG7U

DuBois, W.E.B. (1994). *On the souls of black folk.* New York: Dover Thrift Edition.

Duranti, A. (1997). *Linguistic anthropology.* Cambridge: Cambridge University Press.

Halasz, J. R., & Kaufman, P. (2008). Sociology as pedagogy: How ideas from the discipline can inform teaching and learning, *Teaching Sociology, 36,* 301–317.

Hall, E. T. (1976). *Beyond culture.* New York: Anchor.

Hall, S. (1996). The problem of ideology: Marxism without guarantees. In Morley, D., & Chen, H.-K. (Eds.), *Stuart Hall: Critical dialogues in cultural studies* (pp. 24–45). London: Routledge.

Kalantzis, M., & Cope, B. (2012). *Literacies.* Cambridge: Cambridge University Press.

Laundra, K., & Sutton, T. (2006). You think you know ghetto? Contemporizing the Dove "Black IQ Test." *Teaching Sociology, 36,* 366–377.

Lave, J., & Wenger, E. (1991). *Situated learning: Legitimate peripheral participation.* Cambridge: Cambridge University Press.

Marx, K. (1963). *The 18th brumaire of Luis Bonaparte.* New York: International Publishers.

Maxwell, J. A. (2010). Validity: How might this be wrong? In Luttrell, W. (Ed.), *Qualitative educational research: Readings in reflexive methodology and transformative practice* (pp. 279–287). New York: Routledge.

Tiemann, K. A., Davis, K., & Eide, T. L. (2006). What kind of car am I? An exercise to sensitize students to social class inequality. *Teaching Sociology,* 398–403.

YouthCineMedia. (2013). *Undocubus Puganini Po'kwin.* Retrieved from http://www.youtube.com/watch?v=TihR4NyExJ8

6

•••••

Undertake Observation, Interviewing, and Artifact Collection

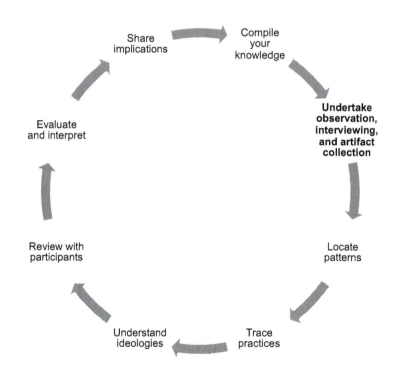

Share implications → Compile your knowledge → **Undertake observation, interviewing, and artifact collection** → Locate patterns → Trace practices → Understand ideologies → Review with participants → Evaluate and interpret → Share implications

•••••

Observing

Observation, of course, involves looking at and really seeing what people do. But that's not all. Observation actually involves all of your senses. Seeing, as well as hearing, smelling, even tasting, and some-times touching, all provide information about people's experiences.

There is nothing like being there.

Hymes made participant observation his hallmark. We will talk more about the *participant* part of participant observation in just a bit. But what it means to really be in a place has changed since Hymes started publishing his ideas back in the 1960s. Think about the affix *trans-*. It means 'across', 'beyond', or 'through'. Many of us live **transnational** lives, with identity ties in more than one national context; many of us live in multilingual communities where we **translanguage**, using all of the communicative resources at our disposal, combining languages in innovative ways. We also have the identity category **transgender**, which refers to people whose internal experience of gender doesn't line up with the gender they were assigned at birth. Now, some people use **trans*** as an umbrella term to refer to the spectrum of gender identities. We are in a moment of time in which **binaries**, either/or and the notion of opposites, are called into question. Perhaps this is a time of both/and.

Additionally, many people spend parts of their lives in **virtual worlds**, or online gaming platforms. Even using everyday technology has transformed our experience of what it means to be in the present moment. Where are you when you are responding to group texts from people who are in different places across the United States or around the world? Yes, you are in a physical place, but you are also in another kind of social space. What it means to be somewhere has changed.

So what does it mean to engage in participant observation? It's a lot more complicated than it seems. What do you actually see? What do you actually hear? It's easy to let your assumptions and judgments get in the way. It can be a challenge to figure out what to observe in a complex situation. Lots will be happening, but you can't observe everything. Our interpretations are always based on what we do observe of and learn from our communities of practice. As Pappas and Tucker-Raymond (2011) explain in the context of their classroom-situated research, ". . . being clear about what we describe (observe) versus what we interpret (infer) is a critical aspect of the inquiry process" (p. 16).

To encourage this distinction, Stone Sunstein and Chiseri-Strater (2012) promote the value for the ethnographer of taking double-entry notes—one set for observations and the other for reflections. They write that these field notes produce an ethnographic analysis that ". . . has two stories to tell: one about the culture and what it means to the informants in that culture, and the other about you as a researcher and how you did your research" (p. 94).

It may be obvious as to what you write on the left-hand side—everything you can in a complex environment where many things are happening at once. But what about the right-hand side? At the moment when you are taking notes, it's likely that you won't have time to stop and reflect very deeply. We recommend that you write down a key word to help you remember what you were curious about when you sit down to revise your notes, soon after you've taken them. Your reflections might be questions about something you didn't understand. They might include things you want to ask about in the future, or they might be reflections on how you felt at the time. You may observe something you think you understand, but you realize in the moment of observation that you may be wrong. The right-hand column is where you will note what you need to ask about the meaning of the event for the person involved. We will go into this in more depth later in this chapter when we talk about how you 'cook' your field notes. Take a look at this framework for double-entry field notes.

What you see and hear	Reflections
Location: Date: Time: Number of people you are observing:	

It's also good to check in about the time as you take notes. We try to write the time on the left-hand side every 10 minutes or so, depending on the context.

Think about this scenario: You are sitting in a coffee shop. You see a woman at a table nearby. She has a cup of what you think is coffee, and she is reading what looks like the *New York Times*. You're not close enough to know for sure. Her cell phone rings. She answers the phone. Her face changes. She starts to cry. She hangs up and sobs. Can your double-entry field notes look like this?

What you see and hear	Reflections
Location: Spirit Winds Coffee Shop Date: 8/8/18 Time: 7:40 AM Number of people you are observing: 9 The woman got some sad news.	I wonder what the phone call was about.

Can we see sad news? We can see and hear someone cry. We can see someone's face change. We can see someone hold a phone to her ear. But assuming that she got sad news, well, that's an assumption. If this observation were part of a larger project, it would make sense to ask the woman about that moment. When you make use of double-entry field notes, you want to record exactly what you see and hear on the left and then, later, write down your questions, confusions, or musings on the right. The right-hand side is also a good place to explore your own assumptions. Your field notes from participant observation need to be richly detailed. These clearly aren't. How would you revise the field notes above? We know you weren't there, but we want you to imagine the situation, so that you can understand the process better.

Your field notes are important documents. They are part of your data. One of the big mistakes people make when beginning to take field notes is not understanding the difference between what they see and hear and their reflections. That's what the example above was about. Be sure to check your field notes to make sure you have really separated your actual observations from your musings. Many times when people begin taking field notes these two categories are blurred. After doing an observation and taking field notes you need to turn them from 'raw' into 'cooked' within 24 hours. Why 24 hours? Because your memory is likely to play tricks on you if you wait any longer. You may incorporate understandings that you have gained since that observation into your old notes, and you really want each observation to be its own record of the event and your understanding of it at that moment in time.

What exactly are **raw** notes? If they are handwritten, they may be nearly illegible. Char often cannot read her own handwriting. Is this a consequence of using the computer all the time? Probably. If your notes are digital, they may be so filled with typos that they are on the verge of being unreadable as well. Your notes may also be in a mix of languages. But given that you have just come from whatever you were observing, your notes, in combination with your short-term memory, are what you need to help you turn them into data. You need to sit down to **cook** your notes, as we have said, within 24 hours. The experience will still be fresh in your mind, and that's important. When you cook your notes, you start with the left-hand column. You translate your telegraphic scribblings into full thoughts. You thicken the description. Create a picture in your mind of each moment of the experience and write it down. More details will come. This, like everything, is an iterative process. You will read and re-read the left-hand side, adding more detail, incorporating things you were aware of but left out because of time. Once the left-hand side has been expanded, you read it again and reflect on it. Now you are beginning to cook the right-hand side of your notes. Are there questions that arise as you read the left-hand side? Things that are unclear? Things you want to ask people about or check on? Feelings you had while doing the observation that you want to record? Now is the time to expand the column on the right-hand side. That's what it means to cook your raw field notes. If you don't cook your notes right away, to continue with the cooking metaphor, your notes spoil. That is, if you wait a week or a month to cook your notes, they won't make sense to you. We are the voice of experience on this point. Drop everything and cook your notes!

Observing People's Everyday Practices

Find a place where you can sit and observe people without being obtrusive. Possibilities might include the school cafeteria, a coffee shop, the library, a shopping mall . . . you will come up with the right place. Use either a laptop or old-fashioned pencil and paper. Begin by taking raw notes; jot down whatever you can scribble or type in the moment. Your cooked notes are the ones that you put into the double-entry field note format above. They have a chance to simmer for no more than 24 hours before you (1) enter them as observations in the left column and (2) react to them reflectively in the right column. Don't try to include the reflections in the moment (although putting a note to remind yourself of something helps at the time). Reflect on what you've seen and heard when you put your notes into the double-entry format.

Share excerpts from your field notes with the class.

When you type your field notes into the double-entry format, it probably feels cumbersome to you. We understand. We promote the double-entry field notes model as a tool for learning to separate your musings from your detailed description of what you see and hear. Once you have learned to separate the two kinds of perception, you can give up the double-entry model. It came from the time when the only option was to hand-write field notes. Char likes to embed her musings and questions in the body of her notes, but she puts them in another color. You will see examples of how other people take field notes in the coming chapters. You will find a way that works for you.

Now that you've had an informal experience of observing people from afar, let's look at one application of participant observation that typically happens outside of academia: consumer research.

Ethnographic Practice: Dos and Don'ts

Watch "What People Are Really Doing" at http://blog.usabilla.com/top-ethnographic-research-videos/. You will hear from a number of design ethnographers at the Illinois Institute of Technology Institute of Design about the how-to's of their fieldwork. One application of ethnography outside of academia is consumer research. Ethnographers go into homes and work-spaces to observe and interview people as they go about their daily activities. For design ethnographers, the goal of this research is help develop new products or environmental designs that make life or work more productive and/or enjoyable. As you prepare to watch the video, fill in the columns below with what you learned from the video.

Ethnographic Practice: Dos and Don'ts

Do	*Don't*

●●●●●

Recording Events and Interviews

With your participants' permission, of course, you may be able to audio- or video-record events and/or interviews. You will still take thorough notes while you record the interview or event, but with the knowledge that you have recorded what's going on, you will be more able to focus on what is happening or being said. During your observations or interviews, because you may have difficulty keeping up with the flow of activities, recording will help you later fill in what you may have missed seeing or writing down. That's one scenario. Sometimes it works in the reverse—having taken notes can help you decipher the context of your recording. It depends. The notes you take while recording should help you recreate the context in your mind.

During your interviews, recording allows you to listen more fully to the participants' responses and to more easily ask relevant follow-up questions. It's also how you create your transcripts, which are the basis of how you come to understand your data. It's important to stay in the moment and really listen to what people say. That is, you don't want to be thinking about what your next question will be while the participant is answering your previous question. This can lead to the participant not feeling listened to, which is something you don't want to happen. If you are able to record and take notes, it's good practice to periodically record the time in your notes so you will later be able to match your handwritten or digital notes to the recording.

But always be sensitive to the feelings of the participants in your study. Remember, you can only record interviews with people's permission. In Char's work with undocumented migrants, some people refused to be recorded. They explained that because their lives were so much under surveillance, they wanted their homes to feel safe and to be the place where they were in charge. Of course, Char agreed and, instead of recording, took extensive field notes. The people in your study have very generously agreed to invite you into their lives. Be respectful of that.

●●●●●

Interviewing

In the video you just watched, notice that the design ethnographers asked the participants questions. Asking questions is key. The ethnographic interview is a way for you to gather data and get to know the people in your study. It is a chance to learn more about what people know, what their opinions are, and what their values are. It's a way to start uncovering their ideologies as well. Interviews offer people an opportunity to reflect on their own practices, and often we can learn things we could not learn through observation alone. Conducting interviews along with participant observation is key. It's common for people to present their ideal selves in an interview, but as you observe them in their everyday lives, you may find another story—what they do and what they say they value don't always line up.

For example, if you were to ask Char about how she eats, she would go on and on about all the healthy foods she eats as a mostly vegan vegetarian. She loves kale and legumes and all those kinds of healthy foods. And while she mostly eats a healthy diet, if you were to spend the day shadowing her, you might be surprised to see her eat some chocolate. And while one day it might be 70 percent cacao dark chocolate, another day it might be a Heath bar. It's not that she is lying in the interview; it's that she's foregrounding some things and backgrounding others. Please don't judge the people in your study if and when this happens. It's something almost all of us do. It's common for people to present their ideal selves in a formal interview. That's why relying on interviews alone doesn't lead to the best data. **Triangulation**, gathering data from three or more sources (e.g., participant observation, interviewing, and artifacts or documents), is a powerful way to increase the trustworthiness of your data.

Often, ethnographic interviews are conversational. The more people talk, the more you learn. But sometimes the interviewee will wander off topic. If this happens, it's usually your job to gently bring them back. However, that digression may inadvertently show you something important that you never thought to ask about. It's also possible that things come up in interviews that bring people back to painful experiences. Char was conducting an interview about a participant's education, work, and migration experiences. When they talked about her school experiences, the participant was brought back to her childhood and to experiences of sexual abuse that she had shut out of her mind for a long time. She described the abusive experiences, her shame, and her deep sorrow. She cried. This is when you need to be present with another human being and listen empathically. It's not the time to worry about your recording equipment or to guide the person back to your question protocol.

Most of the time, ethnographic interviews show compromise; they are semi-structured. That means you come with a list of questions or topics you want to find out about, but you . . . remain open and let questions come from the context. It's also good to go with lots of . . . open-ended questions, such as "Tell me about how you started this business" or "Describe what happened when you crossed the border." Asking people to describe an experience is usually very productive. Don't be afraid to ask additional questions or check for clarification as you go along. Be an active listener. Maintain appropriate eye contact, taking cues from the other person, even though you will also look at your questions, your recorder, and your notes from time to time. Nod. Say 'uh huh' or 'hm hmm' once in a while—naturally—to show you are actively listening. This is what discourse analysts call backchanneling. It makes an important positive contribution to your interview. But also be conscious of your own responses. When Char conducted her first recorded interview, her responses of "wow" were peppered throughout the recording. Use backchannels, but be conscious of not overusing them.

Most important, be natural in your interest. Act as you do when you are listening to people who have something to share that you find instructive and significant. Take your cues from the people you are talking with. Listen and follow up when they have something to say. Ask more questions when there is more you want to know. And while we have talked about the ethnographic interview being conversational in tone, remember that the interviewee should be talking the most. You can make comments and even share similar experiences you have had, but you always need to remember that your job is to get the participant to talk.

●●●●●

Finding Your Questions

Of course, each research context is different, so we can't tell you what specific questions to ask. You may be trying to understand a community of practice, or you may be trying to answer a question about people's experiences, practices, or ideologies. You may be trying to understand people who are at the center of a community, the periphery, or both. You may be focusing in on relations of power. This approach to the ethnography of communication is big enough to incorporate all of these possibilities.

But the question remains . . . how do you ask questions? The particular questions you ask will vary, and once you are in the field, you will learn how to ask better questions as you spend time with people. But you need some questions to list on your IRB proposal ahead of time so members can understand what kind of questions you will ask, and to get you started once you enter the field.

We like some of the ideas that McCurdy, Spradley, and Shandy (2004) have about asking different categories of questions, such as the grand tour question, the mini-tour question, and the example question. They have given names to practices you probably already have in your repertoire. **A grand tour question** is a descriptive overview question. It's like asking, "Could you show me around?" If you're conducting the interview away from a community context, you can also ask people to imagine their space and take you on an imagined tour. That's a grand tour of space. You can also ask them to give you a descriptive overview of actions. You might say, "Take me through what you do on a typical day, from the moment you wake up until the moment you go to sleep." Grand tour questions help you get the lay of the land, in terms of both space and practices. They are a great way to get people to describe what they do. If the information you get on your first visit isn't too detailed, don't worry. With time, as people get to know you better, you will get more information. You will also learn to ask more specific questions as time goes on, because you will know more about what you don't understand.

McCurdy, Spradley, and Shandy (2004) also encourage new researchers to ask people to describe their experiences, rather than asking directly why they do the things they do, especially at the beginning of a project. For example, Char used to work at a school where everyone called the break room the blue room. It turned out that the room had once been blue, but it had been painted over long ago, so that all the walls were now White. But it was still called the blue room. Most of her co-workers hadn't been at the school when the room was blue, and they didn't know why it was called the blue room. To them, it was just the name. And if someone had asked them why that White room was called the blue room, they might have felt uncomfortable saying they didn't know. Sometimes you have to hold on to your "why" questions for a while. You will learn to ask questions about why things happen as time goes on.

Mini-tour questions are a way to ask questions about a particular practice or ideology. They come from what people have already told you, and they allow you to inquire about something you need to understand better. For example, Char was doing a study in a rural area of western Mexico, and after she had been there a while, two young people who were friends of the family she was staying with migrated to the United States, without documents, to pick apples in Washington State. Before the young people left, the family Char was staying with pointed out a man at the market who was the *pollero* (a human smuggler) in their community, noting that he had helped the youth get to the United States. Char had heard people talk about *coyotes* (another word for a human smuggler) along the border, and she wondered whether there were differences between these two terms. She asked a mini-tour question like this: "Could you describe to me what a *pollero* does?" After she got a response, she asked, "Now, could you describe what a *coyote* does?" This started a conversation in which many people offered their opinions. This conversation resulted in people deciding that although both are terms for human smugglers, a *pollero* was someone in this community whom people knew and trusted. But a *coyote* was someone along the border, who wasn't known or trusted and was probably more dangerous. That's an example of a mini-tour question. That question couldn't have been on Char's IRB proposal because she didn't know to ask it until she was in the field.

The final question type that will help you as you start out in the field is what Char and Judy think of as **an example question**. It's the same as what McCurdy, Spradley, and Shandy call a "story question" (2004, p. 40). It's a question category in which you ask for an example or a story. So, after Char asked a mini-tour question about the difference between *polleros* and *coyotes*, she asked the group whether they could give her examples of interactions they had had with each kind of person. The stories and examples went on late into the night.

● ● ● ● ●
More Question Types

One of the question types new researchers often ask falls into the category of the **leading question**. Leading questions can easily sneak into our repertoires. Beware! They are questions that, often without your awareness, guide the interviewee to a desired response. "What do you like about the field of engineering?" or "Tell me about your favorite parts of this poem" sound innocent, but they are not. There are assumptions lurking in these questions that someone likes engineering and that they have favorite parts of the poem. Leading questions taint your data. You can neutralize them by rephrasing your questions as "Tell me about your experiences in the field of engineering" or "Tell me what you think of this poem." The differences are subtle but very important. When you have a question protocol prepared, be sure to check it for leading questions. And when you're in the field, asking questions spontaneously, be sure to monitor yourself for leading questions.

Sometimes you will ask direct questions, and sometimes you will ask indirect questions. It depends. Sometimes you will ask questions about something you noticed while you were observing or about something you didn't notice but were told about. There are many "why" questions you cannot answer through observation alone.

Here's an example. In her work with undocumented people, Char observed one of the women in her study wearing brightly colored clothes at home and in the neighborhood but selecting black, blue, and brown clothes when she left her neighborhood and went to work. Char observed this pattern while they were folding laundry together but didn't know whether it was meaningful. She asked about it and found out that this was a very conscious choice on the part of Rosenda (a pseudonym). Rosenda thought that she looked more Mexican in bright colors and that it was dangerous to look too Mexican in public. She saw "Americans" as people who wore black, blue, and brown, and so she wore these colors for what she perceived as protection. Char might have thought this was just a personal preference if she hadn't asked.

There are also questions that involve patterns we may not have enough observational data to confirm but yet wonder whether they exist. Char had spent time in the homes of many people who owned the English language program she was inquiring about, and almost all of them were struggling economically. The people who were struggling all displayed the program prominently in their homes, usually above the television. Only one person she visited lived in a middle-class neighborhood, and she was the only person who had the program hidden away in a bedroom drawer. Char wondered whether this was the beginning of a pattern. That is, if, as she suspected, the program represented migrants' investment and striving in the United States, perhaps people stopped displaying it once they were well established. But she did not have enough observational data to make this claim.

Finally, there are questions we ask to confirm the inferences we make about people's ideologies and practices. Judy asked questions of a few of the Muslim women who were her linguistics students about why they wore the hijab. She reflected on her assumptions before she asked them questions. Her guess was that their reasons might be much like those of some Orthodox Jewish women who cover their hair. Judy's assumption was that women wear the hijab to conform to their community's standards of modesty. But that was just one possibility. Upon asking, however, Judy found that—again, much like for Orthodox Jewish women who cover their hair—there are many reasons women wear the hijab.

Judy's students who talked with her about the hijab were Algerian and Saudi women in their 20s and 30s, who were working on their master's degrees at Judy's university. The Algerian women told Judy that their Islamic religion and belief system led to their wearing of the hijab. One woman said that wearing hijab means one follows the beliefs of the Islamic religion and abides by what is written in the Quran. She added that the hijab is mandatory for Algerian Muslim women both as a dress code and as a reflection of religious and national identity. Another woman said the hijab is "protection to women to preserve their beauty". She clarified that a woman's beauty is to be protected from the outside world and kept private for her husband. Another woman commented, "We have to talk about what is hijab first. Because hijab as it was said in the Quran is wearing loose clothes that will not show the body of the woman." As you can see, there are a lot of reasons the Algerian women mentioned for wearing the hijab. But they didn't think about it exactly the way Judy thought they would. Judy thought they would say they wore it because of community standards of modesty. While that was implied as one of the reasons, the women also talked about their identities as Muslims and as Algerians.

Another of Judy's students is from Saudi Arabia, and she expressed similar ideas about the hijab representing her Muslim identity. But she focused more on the hijab as a symbol of her religious devotion. She said, "Since we have to wear the hijab when praying to God, I feel that whenever I go outside wearing it that I'm constantly connected to God." She also noted that she feels more comfortable talking to men when she's wearing the hijab because she knows that her appearance won't be a distraction for them. "Also," she explained, "I feel free when I'm wearing it because I don't have to be obsessed with my body or my hair. I just make sure to dress moderately and nicely and that's it!"

So this woman talked about the hijab as part of her religious practice and about how the hijab made her feel more at ease talking with men. And, finally, she explained to Judy that wearing the hijab made her feel free. She commented that many non-Muslim women are surprised when they hear that.

This is a great example of how we need to continually be conscious of what our assumptions are and that we need to not assume we understand why people do things. It also shows that there are often multiple reasons people who are in one kind of community do things and that we can never assume there is a single reason for a particular practice that applies to everyone in a community of practice.

• • • • •

Collecting Artifacts

Ethnographic research is a triangulated process (Denzin, 2006). Data from three sources is typically brought together to provide a more complete view of a community's ways of knowing. Along with participant observation and interviewing, then, we need to add community documents (e.g., zoning laws, contracts, mission statements) and artifacts (e.g., photographs, homework assignments, writings, drawings). Documents and artifacts might include many possibilities beyond these examples. Cintron (1997) analyzed a collection of false legal documents one of the people in his study possessed—a man who had been undocumented for many years but later had acquired legal documentation. Any kind of physical object might provide information about participants' knowledge and interests. About the significance of document and artifact analysis in the context of ethnographic analysis, Hammersley and Atkinson (2007) write:

> Documents can provide information about the settings being studied, or about their wider contexts, and particularly about key figures or organizations. Sometimes this information will be of a kind that is not available from other sources. On other occasions they may provide important corroboration, or may challenge information received from informants or from observation.
>
> (p. 122)

Documents are often from informal sources, such as letters, emails, journals, drawings, and artwork, that people produce on their own. But documents might also include classroom assignments at a school, memos written by office workers in a business, or the mission statement of a non-profit organization. You might design your study so that you include people's Facebook pages as a data source. Listen to and watch what happens in your field sites. We can't tell you what documents or artifacts you need to collect. Rather, we can just give you ideas about how to look. Each document or artifact, because of its design, use, and purpose, provides further information about how members of the community interact with one another and within the community as they demonstrate their cultural knowledge and skills. They may also help you understand the larger context of people's lives and your research question.

One of Judy's early ethnographic adventures was in a suburban Chicago shopping mall where she took on the investigation of shopper behavior. Along with observing shoppers interacting with sales personnel and one another within and outside of stores, as well as interviewing both shoppers and store employees, Judy's team of investigators gathered together the mall map and all of the store flyers, and they photographed, with permission, store and mall windows and store displays. These documents made it possible for Judy's team to locate a pattern in the mall's layout of stores—those with pricier goods were grouped at one end of the mall, and those with less expensive goods were grouped together at the opposite end. Judy's team wondered whether this layout was intentional so as to make stores selling similarly priced merchandise easily accessible to the greatest number of patrons. They were right. Thirty years later, as we have all become more aware of retail marketing techniques and of our own shopping habits, this is not a surprising finding. However, having the documentation in the form of what they saw, heard, and read during their time in the mall—for example, something as simple as the difference in merchandise cost as printed on store clothing tags—provided evidence to support what would otherwise have been just a hunch.

We all have artifacts. Linguistic anthropologist Lanita Jacobs-Huey saw many meaningful artifacts, such as combs, brushes, and picks, in her 2006 study *From the Kitchen to the Parlor: Language and Becoming in African American Women's Hair Care*. What do objects mean to the people who use them? What is their history? Artifacts that are imbued with meaning and historical significance are called **material culture**.

What do we mean by collecting artifacts? While archaeologists spend their time touching, measuring, and hypothesizing about material artifacts—be they ancient tools or even skeletons —as ethnographers of communication we focus on the meanings people give to objects right now. For example, imagine meeting a man with an intricate and colorful sleeve tattoo. There are two images that predominate: the *Calavera Catrina* and a green-and-white road sign for Texas State Highway Loop 375. The Catrina is a common image in northern Mexico and the American Southwest. She is a female skeleton wearing an upper-class hat, and she is a symbol of death. Highway Loop 375 is a dangerous patch of road in the El Paso area where many car accidents happen. It turns out that this man's mother died in a car accident on Loop 375, and his was a memorial tattoo. That tattoo is an object filled with history and meaning. Of course, you can't collect it. With permission, asking about it and taking a picture of it might be a good thing to do. But it may also just be something important to talk about. One way to "collect" it would be to write about it in your field notes. In your field notes, be sure to include where the artifact was located, who used it, and how it was used.

Finding Artifacts Where You Least Expect Them

Work with a partner. Look at your partner with an ethnographic eye. Are there aspects of his or her dress that might be symbolic or that reflect aspects of identity? A necklace? A ring? A tattoo? A style of make-up? A T-shirt? A button?

Ask questions about their artifacts.

●●●●●
Evaluating and Interpreting Your Data

What does the data you collect *mean*? That's the $64,000 question. You establish relationships with people, you do participant observation, you conduct interviews, you gather documents or artifacts, and then what? You identify patterns, and you interpret what you see, making connections to social theory. It's easier said than done, but it's do-able. Remember, you're not the first person to be curious about the social world. Everyone and everything are always already part of the flow of multiple histories. There are lots of theoretical works and empirical studies that use theory out there. That's why you have a library card. It's more than likely that what you are interested in is connected to things that have already been thought about. It is your job to use social theory to help you interpret your data and to situate your study in relation to other empirical studies that have been done.

Now just because something has been thought about before doesn't mean your study is useless or redundant. *Au contraire*. You are gathering data in a particular moment in time, in a particular place, with particular people, and . . . *you* are doing the work. Those things make your study unique. And the kinds of theoretical frames you use to make sense of your data are going to be specific to you as well. The ethnography of communication begins with identifying a community and a question or topic, and then moves on to compiling your knowledge, gathering data, finding patterns and themes, and then using social theory to interpret the meanings of what you have found. We will explore the ways in which you might interpret your data in Chapter 9.

Wrapping Up

Do you still have questions about interviewing, participant observation, and document/artifact collection? This is the time to think about your concerns and questions. We are halfway through this book, and you should have the following things ready or in process:

1. Permission to study a community or communities of practice
2. A question or topic that you are exploring
3. An approved IRB proposal

Now it's time for you to go out into the field and collect data. Here is a checklist to help you prepare.

Checklist for the Field

Do you have:

☐ The overall questions or themes of your study;
☐ Informed consent forms (both pre-signed by you, one for you to keep and one for the interviewee to keep);
☐ A tape recorder and/or video recorder;
☐ Fresh batteries;
☐ More fresh batteries;
☐ A laptop (depending on your field site);
☐ A notebook (depending on your field site);
☐ Pens and pencils;
☐ A pencil sharpener;
☐ A camera;
☐ Fresh batteries for the camera;
☐ More fresh batteries; and
☐ Your list of initial questions for each person?

This article and others that appear in various chapters as examples of ethnographic inquiry can be accessed through your university library, and the information you need to search for them is available in the References section at the end of this chapter:

•••••

References

Cintron, R. (1997). *Angel's town: Chero ways, gang life, and the rhetorics of everyday life.* Boston: Beacon.

Denzin, N. (2006). *Sociological Methods: A Sourcebook.* Edison, NJ: Transaction.

Hammersley, M. & Atkinson, P. (2007). *Principles in practice* (3rd ed.). New York: Routledge.

McCurdy, D., Spradley, J., & Shandy, D. (2004). *The cultural experience: Ethnography in complex society.* Long Grove, IL: Waveland.

Pappas, C. C., & Tucker-Raymond, E. (2011). *Becoming a teacher researcher in literacy teaching and learning: Strategies and tools for the inquiry process.* New York: Routledge.

Sherman Heyl, B. (2007). Ethnographic interviewing. In Atkinson, P., Coffey, A., Delamont, S., Lofland, J., & Lofland, L. (Eds.), *Handbook of ethnography.* Pp. 369–383. London: Sage.

Stone Sunstein, B., & Chiseri-Strater, E. (2012). *Field working: Reading and writing research* (4th ed.). Boston: Bedford/St. Martin's.

"What People Are Really Doing." Retrieved from http://blog.usabilla.com/top-ethnographic-research-videos/

7

Locate Patterns

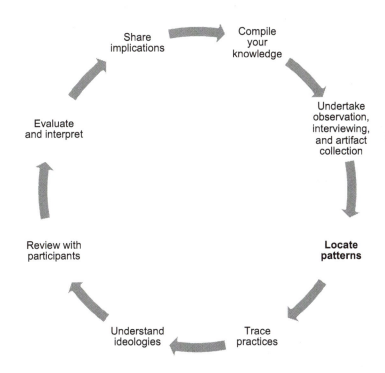

Locating patterns sounds as though it would be easy, right? We follow patterns every day, but we aren't always aware of them. Think about how you get to school. Do you walk? Take a bus? A train? A car? Do you alternate your modes of transportation depending on your class schedule? Your work schedule? Your family schedule? There's a pattern there. Do you take the same route each time to get to school? Or do you alternate routes depending on the time of day and the traffic pattern? There's another pattern. Are your classes online? Do you log in at a certain time or only on certain days? Do you follow a particular sequence in working through the course materials each time you log in? There are patterns here as well.

Uncovering patterns in your data can be a very exciting process. But what exactly do we mean by patterns? Your data has communicative patterns at different levels, so finding a pattern really depends on what level you're trying to understand. We like to think of communicative patterns as existing on three levels. **Micro-level analysis** of patterns considers things like the grammar people use, their intonation, and/or the stress they put on certain words. It also involves looking at the pauses people make in their speech and even calculating the amount of time they pause. What might these things mean? We don't know what goes on inside people's heads. We can only infer what they think and feel from what they do. Does a long pause mean uncertainty in a particular context? Does very quickly uttered speech from someone who typically speaks more slowly signal nervousness? These are possible inferences that might be made at the level of micro-analysis.

Mid-level analysis looks at the content of what people say and do. That is, this kind of analysis focuses on the meanings people make as they communicate in multimodal ways. The emphasis is not on how people speak but rather on *what* they say. Mid-level analysis is sometimes called **content analysis** because it zeroes in on what people say and focuses on interpreting people's content or meaning in context. It is about identifying and interpreting themes in the data.

Macro-level analysis explores the larger social processes that run through your data. Macro-level analysis connects your data (i.e., the data you have already examined at the micro- and/or mid-level of analysis) to larger social processes, or social theory. You will always include macro-level analysis in your ethnography of communication studies. But whether you also analyze your data at the micro-level, the mid-level, or both depends on the literature you've been reading and what body of thought your study is likely to contribute to.

OK. This may seem a bit complicated. Yes, you're supposed to be reading the literature on your topic before you start collecting data. Remember your IRB proposal? Well, you had to write a preliminary literature review there. That situated your study in the literature you had been reading. You need to keep reading more. This is where the good news and the bad news come in. The good news is that scholarly publishing in the United States is vibrant, and that means you are likely to find a place to publish your work. The bad news is that people are publishing new studies all the time, and you need to keep up with what's being written. This can make you feel as if your project will never end, because you have to keep adding to your literature review and reinterpreting your data in light of what other people keep finding. The reality is that once you have finished data collection, you need to analyze your data and share your findings.

Everything we produce represents what we know at a particular moment in time. New studies are underway across the globe at any given moment, and that's OK. Yours will be particular to you and your context. But you still have to keep reading other data-based studies that relate to your topic. However, at this moment in your research process, you shouldn't be reading a lot of social theory. You will have some of it in the back of your mind, of course, but this is the time when you let your data speak to you. This is the moment when you let go of the tight grip you may have had on certain social theories and listen to your data.

When Char was a doctoral student, she had the privilege, along with some of her classmates, of spending the afternoon with a scholar from another university who was giving a presentation on campus. The scholar was Shirley Brice-Heath, a professor whose work Char admired. At the time, one of Char's classmates was struggling with data analysis and asked Dr. Heath for help. Dr. Heath shared that sometimes she read her transcripts again and again, and if no thoughts about the patterns she was seeing emerged, she meditated over the data. The point is that even experienced, renowned scholars know that data analysis can be hard work.

Back to the levels of analysis. The kind of analysis you want to do determines the kind of transcription you will do. Will it be a detailed description of what people say? Perhaps. Especially if you think you might send your manuscript off to a journal like *Language in Society, Discourse,* or *Discourse: Studies in the Cultural Politics of Education.* Will it include some description of the way the words and phrases were said but not be too detailed? That's possible as well. Or will you focus on the content of what people said? These last two levels of analysis are the most common in ethnography of communication. Journals such as *Anthropology and Education Quarterly, Qualitative Research Journal, International Journal of Qualitative Studies in Education,* or *International Journal of Qualitative Studies in Health and Well-Being* are good places for these last two levels of analysis. The fact that you have to make these kinds of decisions before you even start transcribing your data should tell you something.

●●●●●

On Some Level, Your Analysis Begins the Moment You Start Transcribing

In this chapter, we introduce you to transcription. We show you how to transcribe with close linguistic description (the *how*). We also show you how to transcribe for content alone (the *what*). You will decide what level of specificity makes the most sense for your study. After you've been introduced to the first step in data analysis, transcription, then we will show you examples of patterns in different datasets from the three levels of analysis: micro-level, mid-level, and macro-level.

Getting Ready to Transcribe

We're hoping that you have audio-recorded your interviews using a digital recorder. Often, there is a way for you to borrow recording equipment from your university, and this is something your instructor can help you with. While you could use a smart phone to record interviews, review boards look down on this, since the data on your phone isn't very secure. You may also have video-taped events, which would be great. And we hope you have used a digital video recorder as well. Assuming that you have digital files and a software program to help you transcribe with a time delay, or a foot pedal, headphones, and, of course, a computer, you are ready to start. We won't tell you about a specific program to buy, because we all use different kinds of computers and there will be a new, better program by the time this book is printed.

But you might have been perplexed by our mention of a foot pedal. If you haven't done transcription before, we know this sounds odd. But a foot pedal is a marvelous thing, as it allows you to stop the digital audio file at a precise moment, without losing a few seconds, so you don't have to rewind the file all the time. And the fact that you can stop the file with your foot allows you to keep typing. This kind of technology definitely speeds things up. Other programs allow you to stop at a precise moment in the transcript by using a shortcut code.

OK, so you're ready to start transcribing now. But what is it that you're transcribing? If it's an audio-recording, which might mean talk and silence, what is missing? The context. You may or may not have notes about the other modalities of communication that were going on at the moment. And even if you do have notes, it will be hard to match up gestures and other events with the speech that accompanied them. It's not uncommon to be flummoxed the first time you listen to your own audio-recordings. You were there, and yet now what's on the file can seem almost unintelligible. It turns out that utterances aren't the whole of what happens in life. The context has to come back to you. Have your field notes in front of you in order to get yourself back into the context of what happened as you listen and transcribe. It turns out that there is a theory of what's knowable, epistemology, embedded in the practice of transcription. Are you recording exactly what happened and recreating reality, down to timed pauses and intonation, or are you interpreting a part of what happened? We argue that your transcript isn't transparent. Transcription is the beginning of analysis. And that means it's the beginning of interpretation as well.

Over the years, the two of us have learned some techniques that can make transcription a little easier. First, listen to the whole file through your headphones, and make a list of the major things that are discussed, as well as the time codes. It's almost as though you're making a table of contents. This will help you know where things are on the file when you're transcribing. And at this point, you might decide that there are parts of the file that you don't really need to transcribe. You will have a lot of data. It's OK to make decisions about what you will focus on, but don't make those decisions until you've listened to everything a number of times. Once you have decided to transcribe a portion of your data, begin writing down what you hear. This is your second step. Most people like to get the data down without the detailed description just yet. At this phase, it's about getting the content down. The final step will be doing a detailed discursive description of what was said. You may decide to focus on particular sections of the data and only do the detailed description on certain key sections. It's entirely up to you. Again, it depends on what you're looking for. Your final checking of your transcription will always involve reading what you have written while you listen to the file.

In our examples thus far, we have assumed that you're conducting an interview with one person. But you might be recording a group of people as well. **Focus groups** can be a powerful way to get people to talk about shared experiences and to think out loud together. Often one person's point of view will spark that of another, and things will be brought out that might not have been said in an individual interview. Focus groups can be productive and efficient, both for you and for the participants in your study. However, please, please, please don't include more than six people in your focus group. It is challenging to transcribe focus groups because people overlap their speech and it's difficult to know who is talking. Our experience tells us that having two or three people in a focus group usually doesn't produce the magic that comes from five or six people. But more than six can be unruly. And it can be very useful to video-record as well as audio-record a focus group. While the quality of the audio-recording will probably be better than that of the video-recording, having the visual information about who said what will help you determine who is talking when you are transcribing.

What if you are recording naturally occurring talk? Meetings, parties, classes, and cultural events are all possibilities. If you are able to video-record these, that is best, since it can be very confusing to try to transcribe the audiotape. Usually there is overlapping talk or silence, and there are actions you just can't understand through sound only.

• • • • •

What Does It Mean to Do a Close Discursive Description of an Interview?

You have to learn to listen like a linguist in order to hear the differences that you get recorded in a close transcription. Every language-related sound that human beings are capable of making can be described in a transcript. That's amazing, isn't it?

The conventions we present here include multiple modalities (e.g., gestures, space), as well as features such as loudness/softness, speed, pitch, stress, intonation, and silence. When we analyze both the *what* and the *how* of a communicative event, we are closer to the interaction, although, of course, the transcription cannot tell the whole story of what happened.

The transcription conventions we use here were created by Gail Jefferson (2004), who was a pioneer in the field of conversation analysis. Most transcripts that use close analysis of multimodal communication follow some form of Jefferson's system, so you will benefit from learning it. If you find this introduction exciting, you will want to read Jefferson's work, and there are references to guide you at the end of this chapter. Here are the definitions of a few terms to help you understand the transcription conventions:

1. **Turns at talk:** Natural conversation involves an exchange, a back and forth, of contributions by those present. Turns can be verbal or nonverbal; silence can be a turn.

2. **Intonation:** Defined as the vocal pattern or melody of an utterance. There can be sentence-final falling intonation that marks a declarative statement, sentence-final rising intonation to mark an interrogative or questioning utterance, and an increased spike of intonation at the beginning of an utterance to mark strong reaction or emotion such as when exclaiming in surprise, anger, or great certainty or issuing an imperative or command.

3. **Pitch:** Speakers vary an utterance's pitch through the manipulation of their vocal cords. Raised pitch arises out of an increase in the movement of the vocal cords; lowered pitch arises out of a decrease. Fluctuation in pitch can also signal emotion.

4. **Overlapping speech:** While speakers usually time their turns to speak when others are not speaking, sometimes speakers do speak at the same time as one another. This may be a conscious choice or the result of erring in one's prediction of the end of another's turn. Overlap can signal a desire—again consciously or not—to influence another speaker to stop speaking, to indicate agreement or disagreement with the speaker, and/or to assert one's power.

5. **Stress:** The increased force of a given word or syllable in a word. Stress is sometimes referred to as accent by non-linguists.

Transcription Conventions (Adapted from Jefferson, 2004)

[[	Bracket used as a pair, one in each adjacent line, to show where overlap of speakers begins.
=	Equal sign used at the end of one line and beginning of another to indicate that the two lines are a single turn at talk.
. . .	One-half second pause.
(0.0)	Numbers in parentheses used to mark the length of a pause, in increments of 0.5 seconds.
'	Accent mark used to indicate stressed syllable(s) in a phrase, clause, or sentence.
_____	Underscore used to underline syllable(s) with greater than normal stress in a phrase, clause, or sentence.
CAPS	Capitalization used to mark greatest stress on syllable(s) in a phrase, clause, or sentence.
:	Colon used to show lengthened sound. The number of colons indicates relative length.
° °	Degree signs surround utterances that are softly spoken.
↑	Upward arrow means raised pitch.
↓	Downward arrow means lowered pitch.
.	Period means sentence-final falling intonation.
?	Question mark equals sentence-final rising intonation.
,	Comma indicates rising intonation marking a pause within an utterance.
<>	Words within open carets are spoken more slowly.
><	Words within pointed carets are spoken more quickly.
()	Parentheses with no content indicate something was uttered, but it is not intelligible.
(word)	Parentheses around a word indicate something was uttered, but the content is speculative.
(())	Descriptive information about other modalities or noises made by the speaker or in the background.

Working Together

Have two students volunteer to get in front of the class to perform a simple, four-sentence conversation of their choosing. Transcribe what they say using Jefferson's system. When your transcripts are completed, share them with the class. What did you hear? Create a whole-class transcription that incorporates everyone's work.

If this level of analysis piqued your interest, perhaps you would like to listen to a free podcast, Rick Rickerson's *The Five Minute Linguist*. It's at https://itunes.apple.com/us/itunes-u/the-five-minute-linguist/id452255394?mt=10. While the website may look daunting since there are 52 episodes, each episode is—you guessed it—only five minutes long.

Let's look at an example of a close linguistic description of some data. This excerpt comes from a project Char conducted that explored how Latin American migrants form their identities and beliefs about the United States in relation to the English language program *Inglés sin Barreras*. Here, Francisco was talking about using the program *Inglés sin Barreras*:

Interview Location: El Centro, Tucson, AZ

Interviewee(s): Francisco J.

Date: 6/17

FJ: And it's imPOSSible to watch it at [ho:me].

CU: [Oh].

FJ: Yeah . . . uh . . . so . . . and the ba::by watches cartoo:ns, and all that.

Uh, so, no . . . I:: don't watch it.

CU: Oka:y.

FJ: They are the ówners of the TV ((laughs)). =

= Yes, of év:erything ((growling sound)) ((laughs)).

Something Char did here was to break the lines into semantic units. Every time the speaker ended a thought, she moved to a different line to symbolize this. Many times, a close discursive analysis is quite revealing of larger patterns. This brief example gives you an idea of the way you have to listen to your data to get to this level of specificity.

● ● ● ● ●

What Does It Mean to Do a Content Transcription of an Interview?

A content transcription focuses on only the content of an interaction, with limited attention to the *how* of the discourse. Here is an excerpt of a content transcription (mid-level analysis) in translation from a participant in Char's article, "My grain of sand for society": Neoliberal freedom, language learning, and the circulation of ideologies of national belonging (Ullman, 2014).

● ● ● ● ●

Magdalena

1 No me gustaría que se me pase la vida.	I don't want my life to pass by.

2	Si estoy viviendo en este país	If I am living in this country
3	y después siento que es una responsabilidad	and after, I feel a responsibility
4	aprender el inglés.	to learn English.
5	Para ser una mejor ciudadana.	To be a better citizen
6	Para, porque no he perdido las esperanzas	Because, I haven't lost hope
7	en un futuro	for the future
8	estudiar algo y prepararme.	to study something
9	Siento que sería un desperdicio	I feel like it would be a waste
10	hacerme vieja en la cocina,	for me to get old in the kitchen
11	cocinando	cooking
12	aprendiendo nada más de cocina	learning nothing more than cooking
13	y como llevar una casa.	and how to keep house.
14	TENGO QUE aprender.	I NEED to learn
15	Cuando Dios nos dió cerebro	God gave us a brain.
16	Y lo, pudo aprender algo más	And I can learn something more.
17	Y aporta	And to contribute
18	MI granito de arena	MY grain of sand
19	para la sociedad.	for society.

Thinking Together

What do you notice about this transcription? Why do you think Spanish is on the left and English on the right? Do you think numbering each line of your transcript might be useful? Why or why not? Why do you think some examples of close description were included and others were not?

Now that you have a general idea of how to create a transcript, we will move to looking for patterns in data, employing the three levels of analysis we outlined above.

Here Pattern, Pattern, Pattern

Let's imagine that you have transcribed your data. You might wish to maintain it only in electronic form, or you might decide to print it out as well. Now it's time to read through your data. You read it again. And again. Take notes as you read it. What patterns do you see emerging? As a way to practice searching for patterns before analyzing your data, let's first look at some of the patterns in your own life.

Talking Together

Your daily schedule involves patterns. Write down what you did yesterday and the day before, from the moment you woke up until the moment you went to sleep.

Yesterday	The day Before Yesterday
Wake up	Wake up
Go to sleep	Go to sleep

What's the same, and what is different?

Think about your entire week. What activities at which times of day and on which days of the week are patterned? Which things occur and recur at specific times or in some kind of predictable way? And which occur without an obvious pattern in this two-day period?

Share your patterns with a partner.

As we have discussed earlier, the search for and identification of patterns in language use, practices, and our social projects are central to ethnographic work. Patterned behaviors demonstrate the existence of ideologies and practices. They also show us what the norms are in our communities. You may think, "Wait a minute . . . I'm an individual, and my behavior is totally my own." While we all have things about us that are unique, all of us also live in social worlds. Even though we may be unaware of it, those worlds influence our daily lives. The reality is that our behavior is structured by our social worlds while we also maintain agency to do things idiosyncratically. Both things are true.

Working Together

What did you eat last weekend? Talk about it with your partner.

We know that our bodies need food in order for us to survive. But the ways we get that nutrition into our bodies are socioculturally inflected. In the United States, it's common for people to eat three meals a day. (There are, unfortunately, food deserts and economic imbalances that make this far less of a commonality than we would like.) Even given the realities of hunger in the United States, eating three meals a day is a norm, or an example of structure in our daily lives.

Read the article about Rob Rhinehart, who invented the food substitute Soylent, on the following site: http://www.independent.co.uk/life-style/food-and-drink/could-soylent-replace-food-the-drink-that-claims-to-contain-all-the-nutrients-the-body-needs-9334154.html

Make a list of the parts of this story that demonstrate structure (norms). Next, list the parts of this story that demonstrate agency (creative agency). Your examples of structured behavior and agentive behavior are preliminary patterns.

●●●●●
Micro-Level Analysis

Identifying patterns at the micro-level is a way to understand how members of a community use language. Judy audio-recorded and transcribed three interactions among salespeople and customers. This kind of discursive data enabled her to look for patterns in language use among a community of practice in a department store. The data you will analyze here was collected before IRB protocols were in place in the social sciences (that happened in 2004). Today, you would need a signed informed consent form from everyone involved, and it would likely be difficult to get a customer to take the time to read and sign the form. Also, these days, a store would be hesitant to have someone do research if it interfered with business. Read through these three examples carefully.

●●●●●
Sales Counter Data

1. February 6, 1976: Retail department store, suburban Chicago

Customer: ((approaching counter with merchandise in hand)) I'd = = like to púrchase these?

Sales Associate: Súre. Good morning. I'll be háppy to < ring 'em up < for you.

((Enters codes in register. Returns to customer.)) Would you like to = = pá:y with cá:sh, ché:ck, or chár:ge?

Customer: Here's my cár:d.

Sales Associate: Thánk you. ((Returns to register. Enters codes in register. Places merchandise in bag while register is completing the transaction. Tears receipt from register and places it on counter)) Would you please sign hé:re?

Customer: Súre. ((Signs receipt. Reaches for bag.)) Thánk you.

Sales Associate: ((Hands bag to customer)) Thánk you. ((Picks up receipt and gives one copy to customer and places the other in the register.))

Sales Associate: Have a good dá:y.

2. January 7, 1978: Retail department store, suburban Chicago

Sales Associate: ((placing customer's clothing in a bag while another customer approaches the counter)) Goód morning. I'll be wíth you in a móment.

Sales Associate: Thank you. ((As she hands the bag with the purchase to the customer))

((Turns to another customer) How can I hélp you?

Customer: > I'd like to retúrn this please. < ((Places bag on counter)) = = Hére's the receipt.

Sales Associate: Thánk you. OK. Do you have your chá:rge card?

Customer: Yeah. ((pulling cards from wallet)) °I'll get it out of my = = wállet.° Hére it is. :((hands charge card to Sales Associate))

Sales Associate: Thánk you. This will just take a mínute. ((completes transaction at register and then places charge card and credit slip on counter)) Would you please sign hér:e?

Customer: ((Signs credit slip))

Sales Associate: [Tears off one copy of credit slip and hands it to customer. Puts other copy in register] Thánk you. Have a good dáy:.

Customer: hmhmm

3. February 20, 1978: Retail department store, suburban Chicago

Customer: I'd like thís please. ((Puts pair of jeans on counter))

Sales Associate: OK. Good mó:rning. Will that be cá:sh, ché:ck, or = = chá:rge?

Customer: I'll pay by chéck.

Sales Associate: OK. ((Goes to register with jeans. Inserts sales form in register. Enters sales associate code, garment's tag number, and garment's price.))

That'll be twenty dó:llars and forty-nine cénts.

Customer: [Writes check. Hands check to sales associate].

Sales Associate: Thánk you. May I see your dríver's license and a = = crédit card?

Customer: Sure. ((Gives driver's license and credit card to sales associate.))

Sales Associate: Thánk you. ((Writes customer's driver license number on back of check. Writes customer's credit card number on back of check under driver's license number. Returns driver's license and credit card to customer. Returns to register. Enters code. Register drawer opens. Puts check in check slot in drawer. Closes drawer. Receipt prints out from register. Tears off receipt. Folds jeans. Puts jeans and receipt in Tyler's bag.)) [Thánk you. ((Handing bag to customer)

Customer: [Thank yoú:. ((Taking bag))

Learning to Look

After you have read through the interactions, get into small groups.
What do the salespeople say? What do the customers say?
What words do they use? How do they use those words?
When is language used, and how? What do you think the purpose of their talk is?
What do the patterns tell you about salespeople and customer discourse at this store?

The patterns you have identified in these sales encounters probably seem familiar to you (although today many purchases don't need a signature, and there is the difference between credit and debit cards). If you are looking to document and interpret the specific ways people use language in a community of practice, this is how you do it at the level of micro-analysis.

● ● ● ● ●
Mid-Level Analysis

The following field note excerpts are taken from participant observations conducted by Christina Convertino during a three-year ethnographic study. She conducted her study in a large southwestern city, *Sundale City* (a pseudonym) in Arizona, and it focused on school choice, the range of alternatives that families have to traditional public schools in which attendance is usually based on where people live. She explored the cultural production of school choice in the everyday lives of parents, youth, teachers, and community members. Christina was especially curious about how youth invoked the spatiality of school choice to construct identities that defy essentialized and static notions inscribed in dominant social categories, such as "jocks", "burnouts", "preps", and "emos". While two large regional school districts informed this study, the primary research site was a small public non-profit charter high school she calls *Midtown High School* (MHS). A central feature of the school was its curricular focus on place-based education. All names and places are pseudonyms.

You will notice that Christina uses thick description in her field notes, and she includes her own questions, insights, and reflections throughout. Instead of using the double-entry field note style (which is a great way to learn how to take field notes), she put her questions, thoughts, and reflections in italics (which is a great way to take field notes in the field). We asked you to take double-entry field notes as you learned how to separate what you saw and heard from what you wondered about and reflected on. But when you are in the field, it makes sense to take notes the way you see them here (and in following chapters). The examples that follow offer you ways to think about how you will take field notes. You will find a way to do it that works for you. Take time to read Christina's four entries that follow. Each one is from a different week in October 2007.

● ● ● ● ●

1. Participant Observation conducted on 10/03/07 at MHS

"Urbanworks" Class

A year-long required freshmen course that orients students to the place-based curriculum, with particular focus on teaching students how to engage with the public during field-based experiences in the community. I return to school for "Urbanworks" and am shadowing a freshman female who moved here a couple of months ago, recently from Citysville (pseudonym). Her brother attends the school and is either a sophomore or a junior—they don't live together (he lives with the dad) but they get along. She is going to the school because her brother goes. The emphasis of "Urbanworks" for this period is the city as a resource. The teacher tells me the "Urbanworks" for freshmen is about how to act in public, how to solve problems (learn skills) using the city as a resource. 3 themes for the entire freshmen "Urbanworks" are collaboration, communication, and resources. This teacher refers to it as activism. The class is making a large detailed map of downtown Sundale City to hang in the school. The focus is on art, justice, and historic resources. Today, the students go online to look up historical landmarks downtown. They are working in groups and are assigned

3 landmarks to find on *MapQuest* and then to plot on the class map. After we do the in-class work, we go out for a walk to find some of the landmarks. Students are allowed to meet up in the park in front of the public library. Students wander alone or in groups of twos, sometimes larger. They stop at carts on sidewalk (there is farmer's market every Wednesday set up at this location), candy store—down the street and a coffee shop. The teacher waits on the corner for students to finish getting snacks and drinks. Two other MHS teachers approach—one chats for a moment and then goes on to buy some food at the farmer's market. Before she leaves the other teacher (Spanish teacher) asks me about my research. I tell her it is about educational choice. The other teacher says that students have too many choices and then they can just keep choosing out of a school if it doesn't work out. Spanish teacher says even though she works at a charter school she doesn't believe in them. She says these students don't have to do anything, everything is handed to them and everyone caters to them because they have this and that problem at home or with friends but she feels like they just need to suck it up and deal with it. She says it is life and that she had problems and everyone does but you still have to do your job. She compares these kids to students back East and says how unprepared and relatively unskilled the students here are compared to students back East.

After we came back together as a class, we walked around downtown and stopped at the "Presidio" where the student is who is my designated "hostess" said her grandfather had painted the mural. Students generally walk in groups or groups of two. We had a camera from school and female student took photos. *I find it a little awkward (feeling self conscious) and decide not to push conversation with students unless something comes up. I figure it is better for them to just get used to me being there. I am interested in what we are seeing but am also hot and tired of walking. I am impressed that none of the students just wander off. I wonder about truancy and skipping?* At one point, I am walking in the back of the crowd and I see a student stopped in the courthouse passage and he asks me if he can buy a snack and I say yes. When I catch up with the class and everyone is ready to move on the snack kid still hasn't gotten back and I go back to get him and tell the teacher and then when he gets there the teacher tells him to stay with the group and I tell him it was my fault because I told him he could. *It felt awkward at the time and I was afraid of the teacher being mad at me but also hoped that the student noticed that I took the blame. As I write this I realize I need to be careful about not disrupting class flow or rules.* While we are walking a girl asks me what I am doing and I tell her and she says that she has a female relative that did a Masters in education. I ask another kid that ducked at a bunch of flying pigeons whether he has seen the movie *The Birds*. When we get to the historic movie theater downtown *The Birds* is on the schedule and I show it to him. At the Nelson House (a historical hotel and restaurant) we go in the lobby. The teacher reminds everyone that it is a business before we go in and that we need to not be disruptive. We go in building to look at architecture, drink water, and use restrooms. Following we walk several blocks back to school.

●●●●●

2. Participant Observation conducted on 10/16/07 at MHS

"Study Skills": a support class for MHS students with IEPs or 504s.

Excerpt from full day of participant observations in "regular" academic classes.

Sit next to Vance (White male sophomore student) and Matt (White male junior student with Autism)—he is not required to write in most classes. I often see him reading a sci fi novel in class. We are in small classroom with desks set up in a rectangle formation and some desks on side against wall for students who need to work alone. Students are working independently on different assignments. Teacher (White male special education teacher) is moving around room, checking with students and providing one-on-one assistance where needed. Vance and Matt don't have much to work on so they play chess. Vance asks me what I am doing there and I tell him about my research. He tells me that he has switched a lot of schools. He tells me that he is "street smart" not "school smart." He tells me that there is a long waiting list for charter school so students who "get in" get along. It is a big piece for him—"getting along." He cannot deal with classes of 31–40 kids. MHS is small about 175 students—he can deal with this size. He sees all the faces and is more comfortable. He says charter schools are better than public schools. He tells me about his ability to build computer games, take computers apart and build programs. He seems to know a lot about computers. He tells me he will talk to me when it gets time for me to do interviews.

●●●●●

3. Participant Observation conducted on 10/17/07 at MHS

"Urbanworks": Gardening and Sustainability

One of several place-based classes offered to sophomores and juniors at MHS. Students have several options for which "Urbanworks" course they want to take during their sophomore and junior year. Urban-works is part of the place-based curriculum at MHS. During their senior year, students will select a community-based organization for their yearlong senior internship.

Met 10th and 11th grade students (10 total) and two male White teachers at community garden for *Urbanworks* class (focus is on sustainability). Three main groups—grouped primarily by gender—males digging holes for trees that will be planted on Saturday, 10/27. Another group of males working with teacher (Jay) to prep beds. Seeds have been planted at school and will be transferred. Hope to grow enough vegetables to sell at farmer's market on Wednesdays in front of library. Very few females. One White female sophomore, Lily wants to plant a flowerbed by entrance to garden. I met up with everyone by tree, she didn't want to go over to flowerbed area because it was far (approximately 100 ft) and she didn't want to be there alone. I offered to go and we went and pulled up weeds. She is very soft-spoken and was quiet to express her ideas about the bed although she seemed to have a clear idea of what she wanted to achieve. Another female student (*don't know name or grade*), kind of stood around until teacher (Mick) asked her if she wanted to water. Later she helped me pick up plastic water bottles, dump contents and put them in trash. Mick picked up trash along the road—he mentioned something about neighborhood, "see we are doing some good out here" (garden is located in the outskirts of downtown in a low-income area). After about a half hour, a group of 3–4 (F) and 1 (M) students and one teacher from Portage High School (a public charter school for Indigenous students) showed up with shovels and watered their garden, which is set off from MHS gardens. Students were very quiet. Teacher was interactive asked about the MHS garden and said a little about their situation. They came out in a van (looked like a school vehicle—not personal car). MHS kids took city bus and had to walk about 10 mns to get back to bus since there is no school transportation. Jay took bus with them and Mick drove car to carry tools (Vance helped him out). While working together Lily tells me that she was at Carbonaria High School last year but she moved and Rinsdale High School is her neighborhood school. She didn't elaborate on the details. I asked her if she hadn't liked Carbonaria and that is why she came to MHS and she said no, that she had moved. She chose this *Urbanworks* because she likes to garden and has been growing roses since she was 6. She covers her plants when it is cold—she talked about a thermal freeze. She also has a peach tree that the realtor told them to cut down since it draws too many insects. *It was unclear whether or not she has moved to Rinsdale neighborhood or is commuting—seemed like it could have something to do with a divorce or some family issue—she didn't seem too keen to talk about that.* She asked me what I was doing and I told her—she listened with no comments. She is petite, blond (probably dyed), a few piercings, striped shirt, skull belt, skinny jeans, converse. The other female was in more nondescript clothing and more "feminine." Her hair was curled, nails done, she had lotion in her purse, which she put on after cleaning hands. Lily asked if I was coming back. Vance seemed quieter and more reserved towards me that day. I said hi to him and he asked me if I was going to decide if the school was good or bad and I told him it wasn't like that—not a judgment but just trying to understand charter schools. All students seemed to be engaged and working hard.

● ● ● ● ●

4. Participant Observation conducted on 10/22/07 at MHS

"Humanities" Class: Place-Based Unit on Water and Poetry

Visit to Aqua Calme Park—A large park with historical buildings and regular docents who provide information on park ecology and history.

Unit on water and poetry in conjunction with local writing and poetry organization that will facilitate visit at Aqua Calme. To get to park, there are 2–3 vans (rented??) and one car, teacher Jay, who I ride with. On the way to the park, I am sitting up front with Jay and there are 3 students in the back. Jay asks me about my research and I tell him the focus, he responds that philosophically he doesn't agree with charter schools but charter schools are public and they're here to stay. He says that there is great variation in quality and that parents choose. He also says there should be a minimal level for all students (not sure what he means). He tells me a story about a student he taught (*at another charter school??*), whose mom yanked him/her from school because Jay taught about global warming but not about the other side of global warming. Gigi (female student) is in the back seat and has been crying since we left the school. One of the students in the car says that he was at another charter school— "Sundale Accelerated" (I think he may have just come from there to MHS that year). He tells us that at that school, students would take 3 classes/4 months and graduate a year early. He now attends MHS because he moved and it was too far a drive. He said that he had a house in the desert (he is talking to Jay, other male student, Nate and I) that he liked because it had a yard but that was before his dad went psycho. He lives in a house now close to businesses that don't like his music because it is too loud and inappropriate. He seems very knowledgeable about the name of streets/direction, he also knew the VUSD boundaries (largest school district in region). In the car on the way over: Nate asks me if I've been at the school before. I respond "yes, a lot." *I don't know if he recognizes me as the sub from a couple of weeks earlier who he struggled with over him not disrupting class and getting his assignment done.* He and the other male student in the back of the car are listening to headphones for a while and then we are all kidding around. We get lost and Nate makes a joke about hitting people and then he wonders how much rice it would take to blow up a pigeon, he sees a rat in the street, he calls it a "fancy rat." He says that he has a blood type that makes him immune to the black plague. His relatives from Greece and Italy (Europe) and I say the Mediterranean area and he says, "yes." He says he never gets sunburnt. He went to Mexico and got "black." Jeff and I talk about charter schools, and his job. *I don't feel self-conscious.* When we arrive at the park, I go in the "house" with the group of students that are drawing—(supposed to be tied to their poems and to the park). I stay there for the next period as well and draw with both classes. Most students in both classes opt to go outside but since it is really windy a number of us stay inside. Most of the students hurry through the drawing or draw something else (some kind of anime creature that leads to a story about how Keith (male student) actually saw one in Mexico near the farm that his family has). During one of the drawing classes I am listening to and talking to Keith, Si-El and Cammi. Keith and Si-El went to a local public middle charter school with focus on social justice, Piedmont Middle (*later I learn that a fair number of the students at MHS came from either Piedmont or another local charter middle school with focus on Montessori*), they were both at Piedmont for 2 years. Before that Keith was at Axelwood (public district middle school) where he says a lot of kids did drugs, even in 4th and 5th grades. Si-El was homeschooled by his mom before Piedmont. (*Si-El was doing aerials during the first week of school on the day of the scavenger hunt, later I asked him if he was on a gymnastics team or took lessons and he said no. Whenever I see him in school he will say something like, hey I know you. He is often dressed in a very bright tie-dye shirt and is pretty soft spoken.*) Keith continues to tell me that he also volunteers at the Wilderness Museum—his mom used to always go there but he talked her out of going. His hometown is in the mountains of Mexico. Last summer, he was there and 6 coyotes and 2 men were killed by the Mexican abominable snowman—Keith also said that he has a 6th sense. There is lots of joking going on between Cammi and Keith. Cammi is always drawing anime characters. She said that there are 64 characters, 8 main ones. Teacher asked where she learned that and Cammi hesitated and then said "someplace"—teacher touches her back and asks her to do in-class project. Cammi says that she doesn't like when people touch my back and the teacher replies, "you touch my back" and

Cassie says, "I do that to get your attention." At lunchtime, I walk around for a while and then settle at a picnic table with a group of boys. There are 2 or 3 other tables of groups and then smaller couples or trios of students dispersed around the park. One student, a long-haired White male sits alone. Some tables are all male, some mixed, some kids walk off to the periphery of the park. I circle around the park walking and eating my apple. I don't see teachers. I stop at a table of 4 males who are debating whether *Coke* or *Pepsi* is better. I ask one student if he got his soda from the machine at the park and he says "no." I ask if there are any vending machines, they tell me "yes" and that it is a $1.50. Another student says that he wouldn't pay that much. Keith and the other student debating *Coke* vs. *Pepsi* ask me which I like better and I say I used to like *Pepsi* better but now I prefer *Coke*. Debate ensues between 4 guys at the table, also debate other sodas and which is better. At some point, the conversation moves to IQ and they are talking about IQ tests—scores between 150–165. Some of the kids have taken an IQ test and know their scores. They joke when one kid says his score was 200, they say that even Einstein's score was not 200. I ask if they know average IQ and Keith says 150. There is a lot of jostling, cussing and sometimes they look up at me and say "sorry" but mostly they ignore me. I clean out my purse and ask if anyone wants lollipops (*I carry them in my purse for my 2 year old*). Si-El comes over and David doesn't move. So, I move my stuff and Si-El sits down and says, "thanks." Then he says that he has good manners and I say, "yes" and then he also says that he has a good lunch, "well-rounded." Many of the kids don't have lunches—just a drink or nothing. I go to get a soda and when I return, Keith asks David if he knows what a "dyke" is—he says, "yes." Keith asks him what it is and David answers a "woman." Keith tells him to be more specific. Another student says a lesbian and David says "yeah that." Then a debate (led by Keith) starts about refining the definition of a "dyke." Keith says that dyke dresses like a guy and is "goth." The other kid says, "it's like a tomboy." Keith says, no and that "a tomboy is a tomboy." Keith repeats, "a goth lesbian." Throughout the conversation, there are several references to actual mothers as well as frequent use of the expression "your mamma." They have also referred to me as "mothergoose" since I gave them the lollipops. The student with the *Dead Kennedys* sweatshirt says that dykes aren't goth and that they are more punk. Kevin says "same thing." And the *Dead Kennedys* kid replies, "are you kidding?" The debate then moves to the difference between "goth" and "punk." Someone says that the kids at this school are "punk wannabes." Keith names a few bands that he thinks are punk, i.e. *Metallica*. *Dead Kennedys* kid says that's Metallica music and then lists the *Ramones*, *Dead Kennedys*, and other old punk bands. Someone criticizes *American Reject* type bands and kids get defensive (using the expression "your mamma" to communicate their defensiveness). The earlier lunchtime conversation at this table is: do you remember preschool? Keith says he cannot believe it has been 10 years since 1997 and that he was 5. A kid replies, "yeah" and someone would rub your back. And then Keith replies and then "butt fuck you." David says that he failed preschool by not going. They move to talking about the drawings—earlier another kid is teased for failing 8th grade a bunch of times. I laugh at a lot of what they are saying—(*it seems so random but so automatic at the same time*). *Dead Kennedys* sweatshirt kid says that he went to preschool in Mexico and then makes reference to living in Mexico. Kevin says "yeah," I lived there too. At other table, there is a lot more boy/girl interaction. Sara (female student) sits on Nate's lap. Something about going to beat someone up at another table they walk over—Erika (another female student) goes with them to protect whomever they were going to beat up. On the way to lunch, one of the teachers tells me that there was a behavior issue. [*I find out later that there was a problem (discipline) last week so they put a group together that I could be with and referred to it as the "dreamy girls."*] The final class is poetry writing. The class is given some prompts and given the choice to go outside. Most everyone goes outside. I stay inside and take field notes. Towards the end of class, everyone comes in and volunteer to read what they wrote. Erika and Sara are sitting on top of each other (*I often see them entwined or holding hands and wonder about the nature of their relationship*). Erika encourages Sara to read both of hers. On the way home, there is much banter between Jay and Nate about completing assignments or other assignments. Nate is quick and witty in his replies to Jay. There is also lots of talk about music and drugs in the 60s and who overdosed. Nate talks about how his parents took him to lots of concerts when he was a little. On one of the car rides, Nate says that he has issues with his father and wants to borrow a lathe so that he can hurt his father. (*The atmosphere is relaxed and friendly. Gigi seems in a better mood and Nate seems really comfortable around me.*)

Christina's field notes are rich and detailed and give us a sense of her evolving understanding of a complex community of practice.

Now, you are going to practice mid-level analysis. You won't think about the *how* of language here (because it's the language of the researcher, and that would be a different study), but instead you will look for examples of *themes*. Let's imagine that the themes of school choice, place-based education, and youth identities had come up previously in your data. In looking at this data now, you would be likely to notice those themes here as well.

Analyzing Together

Now that you have read these field notes, work in small groups and select one of the themes below. Find all the examples of your theme.

1. School choice
2. Place-based education
3. Youth identities

  Review all of the examples of your group's theme and present them to the class. What constitutes an example of a theme? Can there be variation?
  Is the ethnography of communication approach useful in finding themes within a community of practice? If so, how? If not, why not?

We have seen how micro-level analysis is a way to explore the *what* and the *how* of a community of practice. It's a way to understand what members of a community do with language, and how language intersects with their behavior. In contrast, mid-level analysis is a way to focus on the content of what people say and do. Through a focus on themes that arise from the data, mid-level analysis is a way to understand people's ideas about themselves and the world.

● ● ● ● ●

Macro-Level Analysis

Macro-level analysis is about theorizing the larger social meanings that lie within your data. You will always include macro-level analysis in your ethnography of communication studies. But whether you also analyze your data at the micro-level, the mid-level, or both again depends on the literature you've been reading and what body of thought your study is likely to contribute to.

  The excerpts that follow are from an article Char published (Ullman 2014), again about the *Inglés sin Barreras* project. This is from a section of the article in which she theorized about the larger social meanings of the data. Char didn't know how to theorize this data at first, so she didn't do anything with it for a while. Instead, she started reading social theory and stumbled on the neoliberal theory of people such as Nicolas Rose, Peter Bansel, and Bronwyn Davies, just to name a few. As she read, the data began to make sense. To help you make sense of this excerpt, it's important to know that there was another study participant named Raul who is referenced in this section. Raul's experiences, along with Mirna's, reflected the theme that was being explored (the distraction of parenting). Note how mid-level analysis connects to macro-level analysis in this data.

● ● ● ● ●

The Distraction of Parenting: Mirna

Mirna echoed the same sentiment, that people who do not have success with *Inglés sin Barreras* have somehow used the program incorrectly. Mirna had been in the United States for 18 years when we spoke. She owned a small cleaning business and had come to Tucson from the nearby border city of Agua Prieta, Mexico. She was 37 at the time of our interview and was a single mother with three children. Divorced, she had gotten "custody" of *Inglés sin Barreras* when she and her ex-husband had divided up their belongings. She told me that her husband had gotten the car and she had gotten *Inglés sin Barreras*. One of the few things they had agreed on was that their used car and *Inglés sin Barreras* had roughly the same value.

● ● ● ● ●

Excerpt 4: Mirna

1	Yo creo que el programa es bueno.	I believe *Inglés sin Barreras* is good.
2	Nada mas que a veces	It's just that sometimes
3	uno no lo usa debidamente	one doesn't use it
4	como, como debe.	the way it is supposed to be used
5	Pero para mí	But for me
6	el programa es muy bueno.	the program is very good.
7	La única razón por la	The only reason
8	que yo no he aprendido inglés	that I haven't learned English
9	con el programa	with the program
10	es porque en la casa	is because at home
11	esta uno.	it's just you.
12	Si me propongo una hora	If I try to do something for an hour
13	cada día los niños como ellos saben	every day it seems like my kids know
14	y 'stoy en	and I'm there and it's
15	"MAMI, necesito un vaso de leche"	"MOMMY, I need a glass of milk"
16	Necesito.	I need.
17	Necesito.	I need.

Like Raul, Mirna understood there to be a right and a wrong way to use *Inglés sin Barreras*, and if one has to attend school to learn English, the program must have been used incorrectly. Again, the program itself, its pedagogy, and its significant shortcomings (i.e., its dullness, pedagogical limitations) are erased, and learning English becomes solely a question of personal will. This discourse of language learning, "It's a good program, I'm a bad language learner," was mentioned again and again by study participants. Perhaps the social/economic value placed on the program, through its high cost and high value in trade (e.g., through mutual agreement, this divorcing husband and wife determined that the program's value was comparable to that of a used car), makes it difficult to critique the program. Indeed, suggesting that the program might be less than stellar calls into question the powerful discourse of the autonomous individual who is responsible for consuming wisely. If people must manage themselves as entrepreneurs (Bansel, 2007), the free subject is "responsibilized" (p. 288), and the program (or a school, for that matter) loses importance. It is the consumer, not the commodity consumed, that matters.

It appears that for Mirna, like Raul, the way to "get it right" is to have uninterrupted time to dedicate to using *Inglés sin Barreras* and to have the will to sit through a boring program. The wrong way is to have other obligations, such as parenting, that infringe on the time one can spend working on the program and becoming a neoliberal subject.

Mirna started out by distancing herself from personal responsibility for using *Inglés sin Barreras*, by using *we* to refer to migrants, noting that migrants do not always do what "we are supposed to do", perhaps referencing the social pressure to belong to the United States through the mastery of English (Warriner, 2007). It is significant that she speaks of what migrants are "supposed to do", aligning herself with norms of behavior that involve self-policing. It seems that Mirna is deeply engaged in the process of self-making and is acutely aware of the discourse that says migrants must learn English in order to succeed. But she quickly switched from the distanced *we* = migrants to personalized *I* statements when she spoke of being a mother. Inhabiting her identity as a mother in the first person, it seemed that the parental role was embodied and perhaps in conflict with the more abstract category of the neoliberal subject.

She made clear that her time to study was truncated and that her role as a mother and primary caretaker of her children made it difficult for her to be that profit-maximizing neoliberal subject. Giddens (1991) offers the reminder that while economic and social barriers based on aspects of identity such as gender, age, ethnicity, race, and class were once thought to have been significant, these inequities are now seen, through the neoliberal lens, to be remnants of an almost forgotten past. When Mirna recounted the barriers to her becoming a good neoliberal citizen, she highlighted her children's cries of "I need, I need . . . " Having to respond to her children's needs makes Mirna a compromised neoliberal subject. Hondagneu-Sotelo (1994) critiques the alleged equality of this neoliberal view, offering the reminder that people live in specific social contexts, "not in a vacuum outlined only by huge structures" (p. 187). However, both Mirna and Raul have framed their experiences of using *Inglés sin Barreras* as stories of failure, even though both of them were putting significant work into learning English, as was evidenced by their 20 hours a week studying English at the adult school. But through the neoliberal lens, their failures were (1) lacking the will to learn on their own, (2) allowing parenthood to impede on being "an entrepreneur of the self", and (3) having to resort to using publicly funded ESOL programs to learn English, a collective endeavor that compromises one's personal freedom. Perhaps their sense of failure also came from being embedded in their social worlds and not being able to uphold the illusion of being free subjects who wholly choose their own destinies.

In analyzing this data, Char first looked for themes. She identified six key themes. In this excerpt, the theme being discussed is what it means to be a bad **neoliberal** subject. This example of macro-level analysis started with actual utterances, paying only minimal attention to the *how* of language in the transcription (MOMMY). However, even though the micro-level transcription is minimal, there is micro-level analysis here. She looks at language use by discussing Mirna's decision to use the pronoun *I* versus *we*. Does Mirna put herself in the migrant category? What does it mean that she switches her pronouns? What is the context? Then, these language practices are linked to neoliberal theory, so that this article explores the *what, how*, and *why* of what Mirna said.

Analyzing Together

Work in small groups. Review the excerpt again and work together to complete this chart. Remember, your research might contain a mix of or choice between micro-level and mid-level analysis, but you will always include the macro-level.

How Mirna Said It (micro-level analysis)	What Mirna Said (mid-level analysis)	Why She Might Have Said It (macro-level analysis)

Building Your Ethnographic Analysis

As we end this chapter, it's time for you to look at your own data. What are the patterns you have identified in your data? What are the themes you have found? Write a few of them down and talk about them with a partner.

Looking at My Data

Patterns I Wonder About	Themes I Wonder About

Wrapping Up

As we close this chapter, let's review what we have learned. Using the ethnography of communication approach, we can look at communicative practices at three levels, those of micro-level analysis, mid-level analysis, and macro-level analysis. By learning to transcribe your data at different levels, and then to analyze the patterns at various levels, you are on the road to applying these skills to your own study. We hope you have enjoyed the time you spent with Judy's department store data, Christina's Sunnydale High data, and Char's Inglés sin Barreras data.

This article and others that appear in various chapters as examples of ethnographic inquiry can be accessed through your university library, and the information you need to search for them is available in the References section at the end of this chapter:

References

Bansel, P. 2007. Subjects of choice and lifelong learning. *International Journal of Qualitative Studies in Education*, 20(3), 283–300.

Convertino, C. (2007). Unpublished field notes.

Giddens, A. 1991. *Modernity and self-identity: self and society in the late modern age*. Oxford: Polity Press.

Jefferson, G. (2004). Glossary of transcript symbols with an introduction. In Lerner, G.H. (Ed.), *Conversation analysis: Studies from the first generation* (pp. 13–23). Philadelphia: John Benjamins.

Hondagneu-Sotelo, P. 1994. *Gendered transitions: Mexican experiences of immigration*. Berkeley: University of California Press.

Tannen, D. (1984). *Conversational style: Analyzing talk among friends*. Norwood, NJ: Ablex.

Merrill, J. (Nov, 2014). Could 'Soylent' replace food? The drink that claims to contain all the nutrients the body needs. The Independent. Downloaded from: http://www.independent.co.uk/life-style/food-and-drink/could-soylent-replace-food-the-drink-that-claims-to-contain-all-the-nutrients-the-body-needs-9334154.html

Ullman, C. (2014). "My grain of sand for society": Neoliberal freedom, language learning, and the circulation of ideologies of national belonging. In Blum, D., and Ullman, C. (Eds.), *The globalization and corporatization of education: Limits and liminality of the market mantra* (pp. 87–103). New York: Routledge.

Valdés-Pérez, Raúl, & Aurora Pérez. (n.d.). A powerful heuristic for the discovery of complex patterned behavior. Retrieved from http://130.203.133.150/viewdoc/versions?doi=10.1.1.23.1660

Warriner, D. (2007). Learning language and the politics of belonging: Sudanese women refugees becoming and being "American". *Anthropology & Education Quarterly*, 38: 343–359.

8

•••••

Trace Practices

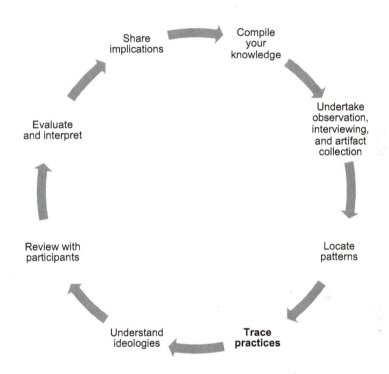

Tracing practices in the ethnography of communication means paying careful attention to what people say and do. Our practices are norm governed (structure), and at the same time, they involve creativity and innovation (agency). This is true for our actions as well as for the ways we use language. The ethnography of communication approach offers a way to focus in on normalized practices (the center) that may lead to group cohesion, to look at practices of outsiders within a group (the periphery), or to look at both the center and the periphery.

As we learn to understand communicative practices and ideologies through ethnographic methods, we interpret patterns through a variety of different theoretical lenses. Sometimes, there is an understanding that the social construction of certain practices is something we engage in as a group, and at the same time, we can critique practices and ultimately change them. And if we change them, we produce new norms. It's seldom the case that everyone in a community feels the same way about all the norms that are in place, as we are all in relations of power. It's common that the people who have the most power in a social interaction have the least consciousness of social norms that benefit them. They are most likely to see practices as "natural" rather than as part of socially constructed practices or norms. Take a look at Krystal D'Costa's blog, 'Anthropology in Practice' at http://blogs.scientificamerican.com/anthropology-in-practice/. Her blog posts, such as the one that follows, share her reflections on everyday practices she observes.

Krystal D'Costa's Blog Excerpt, August 25, 2011

Over the weekend, S and I attended an informal dinner party to celebrate the birthdays of some cherished people in my life. It was a small, intimate affair with four couples of varying ages—the oldest being in their late fifties, the middle two spanning the mid to late twenties, and the youngest on the cusp of twenty. We had ordered in and when the food arrived, it fell to the four women present to put everything into serving dishes and prep the table. The men were occupied with some online endeavor as S had his laptop on the table and was leading a discussion.

We ate. It was a lovely meal filled with the lively discussions that only family members can have when there is little fear about being offensive. Soon, we reached the point where people were sitting back in their chairs with their hands on their stomachs wondering how they would find the energy to move. After a short interlude, one of the young women present took her plate into the kitchen. The oldest woman, whose home we were dining in, rose and cleared her plate and her husband's. As she returned from the kitchen, she said, "Clear the table, clear the table. There are three ladies here who can clear the table." The men, it seemed, were free to continue their discussions.

I felt my face flush with irritation.

Talking Together

1. D'Costa finds herself questioning the norms of one of her communities. What are those norms? How do you react to them?

2. Are there norms in any of your communities that you grumble about? Are there any norms that you challenge explicitly? If so, what are those norms? How do you challenge them? How do others react to your challenges?

If you said that D'Costa questioned the norms because she objected to the women having to clean up after dinner while the men were able to continue sitting at the table, you are on the right track. Later in her post, Krystal explains that it was not the effort of carrying the dishes into the kitchen that disturbed her; it was the expectation that this was a woman's job or duty or role. She noted her discomfort with women and men being obliged to participate in different ways in some communities' activities.

D'Costa reacted with irritation to the expectation that the four women should clean the table because she rejected the gendered norm at play in this situation. The expectations all of us have for ourselves and for others in social interactions are typically not formalized or written down. However, most of us have been socialized in our families, taught either by example or directly to follow particular sets of social norms. All of us have experienced **language socialization**. That is, we learned the practices and norms of our group(s) as children, largely through language. We learn what the right contexts are for adhering to certain norms, and most of us become good at adapting that awareness to new situations.

Learning to Look

In the last chapter, we looked at four sales transactions between salespeople and customers in a department store. Look back at your analysis of the data. What patterns did you find? What do you think those patterns mean?

Salespeople and customers typically greet each other when they begin a sales transaction. Do you see evidence of the salesperson deferring to the customer? If so, why do you think that is?

As we have noted before, there are larger social norms that impact our behavior, even if we are not aware of them. We do not enter into activities as if they are totally new and wonder how to participate. Instead, when we engage in the social world, we rely on what we already know through our schemata. Sometimes, a schema prepares us well for a role. Other times—not so much. It's useful to think of norms as existing on a continuum. Our behavior is structured by the discourse histories that are part of that particular scenario (whether we are familiar with them or not), and at the same time they are available to us to critique, change, and do differently.

Here's an example. When Char began learning Spanish in Merida, Yucatán, back in the 1980s, she learned to say *mande* as a way to say, "Pardon me, or could you repeat that?" Among the people she knew in Mexico, middle-class people in particular considered it rude to say *que* or "what" when they didn't hear something. They used *mande* as a marker of politeness. It is a usage marked by class and nation, and it is a very Mexican term. But when she lived in Ecuador, people were puzzled by her usage of *mande*. It marked her as extra-foreign, and some people critiqued her use of the word, seeing it as a remnant of colonization that people should work hard to eliminate. Because the verb *mandar* means "to order", the word *mandame* literally means "tell me what to do". Often, in global contexts, we are in situations in which multiple norms are at play. And Char's use of the word *mande* marked her as non-Ecuadorian and as someone with a personal history of having lived in Mexico (if people were aware of that connection). We understand the language norms of communities of practice to often be multiple and contested. Understanding how people align their practices to norms certainly matters. But many times, there are dueling norms in a community of practice. Sometimes our work is about understanding the complexity of communities and the ways in which norms change over time.

●●●●●

Identifying Language Practices

Now, let's look as we did in the previous chapter at some ethnographic data. The field notes that follow are those of Katherine Mortimer. She conducted fieldwork in Paraguay, where both Spanish and Guarani, an Indigenous language, are official languages of the country. Katherine wanted to understand how **ideologies** about languages and their speakers were linked to implementation of the national policy for bilingual education in Paraguay.

After reading the introduction to her study, you will read four excerpts from Katherine's interviews with members of the two communities with whom she worked. Remember that your goal here, once you have gotten some background on Katherine's study, will be to look for patterns of practices in the interview excerpts.

Some Background on Katherine's Study

The Guarani Speaker in Paraguayan Educational Policy: Language Policy as Metapragmatic Discourse **(Mortimer, 2012)**

This study was an ethnography of educational language policy implementation in Paraguay. Paraguay has long been known for widespread bilingualism in a colonial language, Spanish, and the autochthonous language, Guarani, but Guarani was not officially prescribed in schools until 1992. That year a new constitution declared Paraguay a bilingual nation, recognized both Guarani and Spanish as co-official languages, and mandated Spanish/Guarani bilingual education for all students throughout the country. This major policy change occurred in a context where ideologies about the two languages, especially Guarani, are complex and contradictory, and so one of my major interests was in how ideologies about languages and their speakers were connected to how the policy was implemented in schools.

Data were collected over 11 months in 2008, as well as during a one-month pilot study in 2005. They included almost 500 hours of participant observation documented through field notes; audio-recorded interviews with 91 individuals, including teachers, school administrators, students, parents, policymakers, and language activists; 28 hours of video-recorded classroom interaction; and policy and school documents, newspaper articles, and student work. Half my time was spent in an urban community at Escuela Coronel Insfrán, where students tended to be Spanish dominant and from middle-class families. The other half of my time was spent in a rural community at Escuela San Blás, where most students tended to be Guarani dominant and from economically disadvantaged families.

Before we look at the four interview excerpts from Katherine's study, we wanted to share an important example of thinking about and respecting the emic point of view in relation to the Guarani language. In Guarani, stress falls on the last syllable as a default. That is, stress can be on other syllables, but it has to be marked explicitly with an accent. Katherine made a decision at the end of her study to write Guarani without an accent when she wrote up the research project, because this is the way that Guarani speakers do it, so it's an example of an emic perspective. She also wanted to avoid exoticizing the name of the language, so that was another factor that led to her final decision about the accent. However, given how Spanish orthographic rules work, when people write about Guaraní in Spanish, they use the accent, because of the rules of Spanish orthography. At the same time, Katherine sometimes wrote Guaraní with the accent in her field notes, because her awareness of this issue was still evolving. If you notice that it is written both ways, that is the reason. Throughout this text, we have suggested that analysis begins the moment you start transcribing your data. Previously, we have focused on how that happens with interview data. It happens with field notes as well, and Katherine's example is a powerful one.

Four Excerpts of Interview Data

Excerpt 1: Profe. Lidia, coordinator of grades 1–3, Escuela Coronel Insfrán (5/21/2008). *This is the urban Spanish-dominant, middle-class school.*

1	Siempre he dicho, digo (tienes una	I have always said, I mean you have a
2	trasformación total que) debe ir	total transformation that the

3 el gobierno, para todos los	government should go, for all the
4 ámbitos, no sé, tratar un poco	sectors, I don't know, to try a bit
5 de mejorar, de lo que era antes	to improve, from what it was before
6 mejoró un poquito, porque antes	it's improved a little, because before
7 no se daba el guaraní, cuando yo	Guarani wasn't taught when I
8 era pequeña ellos no daban guaraní	was little they didn't teach Guarani
9 en la escuela, hablábamos en las	in school, we spoke [it] in our
10 casas pero no dábamos, incluso	homes but we didn't teach it, including
11 en esa época es cuando uno quería	at that time is when you wanted
12 decir palabras en guaraní en la	to say words in Guarani at
13 escuela ehm cómo te digo	school ehm how can I say
14 te miraban cómo	they would look at you like a
15 bichito raro. Y te llamaban	strange bug. And they would call you
16 guaranga y creían que	guaranga and they thought that it
17 era de nivel mas bajo.	[Guarani] was of a lower class.
18 Pero después eso cambio un poquito	But later that changed a little
19 pero hasta ahora ni los niños	but up to now not even the children
20 entre sí, no vas a	among themselves, you're not going to
21 escuchar casi que se utiliza	hear it used hardly ever
22 eso te estoy hablando acá en	that's what I'm telling you here in
23 la parte urbana, que es mas bien la	the urban area, which is more like the
24 parte centro . . . Yo sé que hay	central part . . . I know that there are
25 otras escuelas en los alrededores	other schools in the surrounding
26 que uno va mas alejándose en la	where you go farther out in the
27 parte rural, si los chicos manejan	rural area, yes the kids handle
28 mucho mejor el guaraní, los chicos	Guarani much better, the kids
29 y los adultos también	and the adults too.

Tracing Practices Together

Talk with the person next to you.

Are there things that stood out to you in reading this first excerpt? Focus on the *how* of what people said here. Are you curious as to whether or not the things you notice might be examples of language practices?

Here's a hint: What do you notice about the ways language was used when the speaker talked about Guarani? Perhaps that might be something to pay attention to. Who knows?

Fill in what you noticed about Excerpt 1 on this chart. You'll need to keep building on this chart as you read the other excerpts.

	Ways of Using Language We Are Curious About
Excerpt 1	
Excerpt 2	
Excerpt 3	
Excerpt 4	

Excerpt 2: Directora Felicita, principal of Escuela San Blás (9/24/2008). *This is the rural Guarani-dominant, economically disadvantaged school.*

1	A mí me gustaría que manejen	I would like for them to handle
2	el cien porciento ambos idiomas	one hundred percent both languages
3	porque son idiomas del	because they're both languages of the
4	país, y yo siempre les digo	country, and I always tell them
5	en el lugar donde vayan, ya sea en el	wherever they go, whether it's in the
6	interior, el exterior, siempre tienen	interior, the exterior, they always have
7	que manejar ambas lenguas porque	to handle both languages because
8	como paraguayos se les va a	as Paraguayans people are going to
9	preguntar y les va a preguntar de	ask and they're going to ask them
10	donde vienen y si ustedes no	where they're from and if you don't
11	saben, qué clase de paraguayos van	know, what kind of Paraguayans

12	a ser, a pesar de que el Paraguayo	will they be, despite the Paraguayan
13	tiene vergüenza de haber tenido dos	being embarrassed of having had two
14	idiomas y por qué eso porque	languages and why [would he]? because
15	se le mete en la cabeza que	it was put into his/her head that
16	el guaraní está feo que eso es	Guarani is ugly that it is
17	grosero, no sé si esa parte ya	rude, I don't know if you already
18	investigaste que ellos anteriormente—	investigated that part, that before
19	nosotros no hablábamos guaraní	they— we didn't speak Guarani
20	en la escuela porque decían que	at school because they said that
21	éramos groseros en mi época	we were rude, in my time
22	de escuela era así.	at school it was like that.

Tracing Practices Together

Remember the chart you used after Excerpt 1? Well, your job now is to continue working with your partner and adding to your list of possible language practices.

Here's a hint: What do you notice about the use of the pronouns *nosotros* and *ellos*, or *we* and *they*?

That's just one possibility. You and your partner will find your own possible patterns.

Excerpt 3: Mother of Francisca, 6th grade student, Escuela San Blás (9/4/2008). *This is the rural Guarani-dominant, economically disadvantaged school.*

1	Yo tengo una prima que es guaranga	I have a cousin who is guaranga
2	sabe todito del hasta del	she knows everything right up to the
3	números, guaraní sabe sabe	numbers, Guarani she knows knows
4	manejar guaraní pero bien ( )	how to handle Guarani but so well ( )

5 ella te habla luego así no es	she speaks to you just like that it's not
6 como nosotros hablamos el guaraní	Like how we speak in Guarani
7 por ejemplo ella te dice como *pio*	for example she says to you how *pio*[1]
8 es tu *kypy'y* tu . . . así	is *your younger* sister your . . . like that
9 tu hermana mayor tu	your older sister your
10 hermana menor pero de guaraní	younger sister but in Guarani
11 ella sabe manejar	she knows how to manage
12 *guarani'ete*.	*pure/true Guarani.*

[1] *Pio* is a discourse marker in Paraguayan Spanish and Guarani, derived from the Guarani interrogative *piko*.

Tracing Practices Together

We hope your chart is getting filled in. What stood out to you in this excerpt? Remember, you may not see multiple instances of language use yet. What you're looking for is something that seems unusual or interesting in the *how* of language practice. This is the first excerpt we have seen that used actual Guarani (we've marked it in bold).

Here's another hint: What is the context in which this speaker uses actual Guarani words?

Excerpt 4: Supervisora Gloria, regional MEC supervisor in charge of Escuela San Blás (10/29/2008). *This is the rural Guarani-dominant, economically disadvantaged school.*

1 [El guaraní] es un poco lo que nos	[Guarani] is kind of what
2 identifica, el guaraní es lo que nos	identifies us, Guarani is what
3 identifica aquí en todo el mundo.	identifies us here in all the world.
. . .	. . .
4 Había un momento en que	There was a time when
5 había tanta contradicción en este,	there was a lot of contradiction in this,
6 mis padres, hablando en guaraní	my parents, speaking in Guarani
7 y prohibiéndome a mí, verdad,	and prohibiting me, right,
8 guaranga y maleducada, estás	guaranga and impolite, you're

9   hablando en guaraní, grosera   speaking in Guarani, rude
10 [dijeron].   [they said].

Analyzing Together

You and your partner will complete your chart of possible patterns by adding your thoughts about Excerpt 4 to it.

A final hint: Could the use of *we* and *they* in relation to talking about Guarani be a language practice to investigate? Just a thought.

Now, share your lists with the whole class. Different people will see different things, and that's good.

You just looked at four rather brief excerpts from the many interviews Katherine conducted. Remember, she told us she conducted 91 interviews! And interviews were only one of her methods of data collection. She also did participant observation and artifact collection. Don't think you have to do as in-depth a study as Katherine did. She has lots of experience as a researcher. For most of you, this will be your first experience doing the ethnography of communication. We want you to conduct a smaller study that is do-able for you. Do-ability is important. Do-ability may mean that you will conduct your study over the course of one semester. That's totally appropriate. But it may mean you have to scale down what you plan to do.

What we wanted you to see in examining Katherine's data is that you start to look for patterns by immersing yourself in the data. You don't always know what you're looking for when you start. Your job is to wonder about the how, the what, and the why of what people say and do.

Tracing Practices Together

Now, work with a different partner. Your task this time is to go back and look at the same four interview excerpts but to look for something different this time. What are the possible *themes* you see across the four excerpts? Now you're looking at the *what* of what people say. Use this chart to help you.

	Possible Themes We Are Curious About
Excerpt 1	
Excerpt 2	
Excerpt 3	
Excerpt 4	

Share your possible themes with the whole class.

Tracing Norms Together

Now, work with a third partner. Are you noticing more and more as you read and re-read these excerpts? We hope so. Norms can be an important part of language practices in communities of practice.
   What are possible norms that you see in this data?

	Possible Norms
Excerpt 1	
Excerpt 2	
Excerpt 3	
Excerpt 4	

Share your possible norms with the whole class.

* * * * *

Using Tentative Language

You might be wondering why this chapter has been filled with words like *possible* and *potential*. If you are wondering that, you are paying attention to the *how* of language, and that's good. We want to emphasize that all of the analysis we have practiced and played with in this chapter is tentative, because we are practicing with only a small amount of data. It's not possible to build an argument as to what this data means yet because we haven't looked at enough of it.

* * * * *

Tracing Language Practices and Norms

We hope you have enjoyed the time you have spent with Katherine's data on ideologies about the Guarani and Spanish languages and their speakers. You have practiced preliminary analysis of micro-level patterns and mid-level patterns with this interview data. Is it time to do macro-level analysis? Not yet. We don't have enough of an idea about what's going on with this data yet. We have to spend more time with all of the data, and we have to start reading and thinking about social theory.
   In the ethnography of communication approach, we aren't testing theories. Rather, we are inductively exploring our data and trying to make sense of it. We will think about how to approach macro-level

analysis and how to interpret our data in relation to social theory in Chapter 11. We hope that this foray into Katherine's data will be a model for you when you get to the stage in our model of tracing practices. Remember, this is an emergent process.

Reflecting Together

You have read these four interview excerpts again and again, haven't you? In your ethnography of communication study, you will go over your data from interviews, field notes, and artifacts many times.

Is it useful to analyze data with other people? If so, why? If not, why not?

Are there any possible risks of analyzing your data with other people? What might they be?

●●●●●
Building Your Ethnographic Analysis

As we end this chapter, it's time for you to again return to your own data. What are the micro-level analyses and mid-level analyses that you have done with your data? Have you zeroed in on specific practices in your data? Have you found themes that run through your data? Have you identified norms in your data? Make a three-column list here. In the left column, list the practices you identified in your data at the end of Chapter 7. In the middle column, write one or more themes you have noticed. In the third column, write down the norms you have identified. Are there connections among your three columns? What might the connections be?

Looking at My Data

Practices	Themes	Norms	Connections

●●●●●
Wrapping Up

In this chapter, you have had experience tracing practices. Sometimes it can feel as though you don't know what you're looking for, but that's OK. Tracing practices, themes, and norms is a process that takes time. Even if you are doing a small, very do-able study, you will still have a lot of data to cull through. Don't be discouraged. You will uncover things you never imagined. We are certain.

This article and others that appear in various chapters as examples of ethnographic inquiry can be accessed through your university library, and the information you need to search for them is available in the References section at the end of this chapter:

● ● ● ● ●

References

D'Costa, K. (2011). Clearing the table and holding the door: Constructing social norms. Retrieved from http://blogs.scientificamerican.com/anthropology-in-practice/2011/08/25/constructing-social-norms/

Mortimer, K.S. (2012). *The Guarani speaker in Paraguayan bilingual education policy: Language policy as metapragmatic discourse.* Unpublished PhD dissertation: University of Pennsylvania.

Mortimer, K.S. (2013). Communicative event chains in an ethnography of Paraguayan language policy. *International Journal of the Sociology of Language,* 291, 67–99.

9

• • • • •

Understand Ideologies

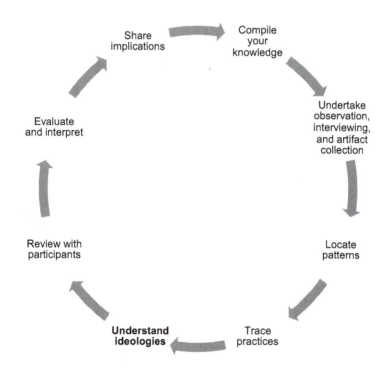

Share
implications

Compile
your
knowledge

Undertake
observation,
interviewing,
and artifact
collection

Evaluate
and interpret

Review with
participants

Locate
patterns

**Understand
ideologies**

Trace
practices

As we continue along the CULTURES ethnographic research cycle, we arrive at another component that can be said to lie at the roots of why we engage in ethnography of communication research. When we as ethnographers attempt to understand behavior, we are looking for the meaning of why people say what they say and do what they do in a community of practice. How does what the participants do and say reveal what is important to them and to their community? Or we could conceive of this step in the ethnographic process as how people's language use and actions inform us—both as scholars and along the continuum of insider/outsider identities where all of us exist—of what people believe and who they are. This chapter is about exploring people's ideologies.

The concept of ideology has a long and rather sordid history, as we've said before. It used to mean "false consciousness" in a classical Marxist way of seeing the world, but now it is no longer a pejorative term. *Ideologies* today refers to people's beliefs about themselves and about the world. They include their philosophies about how society works, including things like the right ways to use language. Your job is to describe and interpret what people say and do. Ethnographers don't participate in a community of practice to tell people what they should do. Instead, we enter communities as learners, trying to understand people's practices and ideologies. Our interest is in what community members themselves value or what they find important in their own communities. Hammersley and Atkinson (2007) acknowledge the role of this component of ethnographic analysis when they write about ideologies, discussing them as "values [that] refer to the human potential that is built into the unfolding of history. . . . Moreover, they provide the key to any understanding of the nature of current social conditions, their past, and their future" (p. 13). Understanding ideologies is no small order.

In this chapter, we consider the multiple and often conflicting ideologies that guide what people engaged in a given community of practice say and do. This is a fascinating exploration because, first, it allows us to recognize that surface behavior is influenced by underlying forces. Like a tree, the branches of actions and interactions are fed by the roots. As those roots provide the nourishment for the rest of the tree, so our beliefs about the world, our ideologies, are what feed our daily practices. Second, understanding the ideologies that guide practices allows us to learn about larger social processes and to do macro-level analysis. When we begin to understand the ideologies that underlie practices, we are exploring the *why* questions of social life.

Let's return to the Paraguayan examples from Katherine Mortimer's data about the ideologies of Spanish and Guaraní speakers and their languages. Language ideologies are the beliefs we have about the social uses of language, and they are an especially rich topic for us to explore with the ethnography of communication approach. We are delighted to continue sharing this data from Katherine's larger study, *The Guarani Speaker in Paraguayan Bilingual Education Policy: Language Policy as Metapragmatic Discourse* (2012).

What follows are excerpts from Katherine's field notes. The data she included was in both Guarani and Spanish, but she has translated her field notes for us here. It may help as you read to be aware that the bold type in each data excerpt presents the participants' utterances in Spanish. The phrases are followed by translations enclosed within single quotation marks. Katherine wanted to record the exact words people spoke as best she could. Your field notes are a written record of things you have seen and heard, informal conversations, and experiences you have had in the field. In Chapter 6, we showed you a model for double-entry field notes, where what you see and hear is in the left-hand column and your questions, reflections, and confusions about what you have experienced are on the right. This is the classic way to take field notes, and it's good to learn to take notes that way, as it reminds you to separate what you see and hear from your thoughts about what you've seen and heard. It can be difficult to master that distinction. However, when you saw Christina's field notes, you noticed that rather than using a double-entry format, she put her thoughts, feelings, reflections, and questions into italics. In the excerpts of Katherine's field notes that follow, you will see she does not use the double-entry method either. You will also see that these particular excerpts don't include reflections, questions, or confusions. That's OK. Both Christina and Katherine have lots of field notes, and their questions, reflections, and confusions run through them. We wanted you to see that each of them has a particular style of taking field notes. While we wanted you to learn to take field notes with double-entry field notes, we also wanted you to see two different ways that people take field notes in real life. You will find your own way, and it depends on you and the context in which you are working.

Look at these five excerpts from Katherine's field notes. They document informal conversations she had in the field but didn't record. That is common in field notes, and you saw that in Christina's notes, too. As you work through these five excerpts, think about language ideologies. What do you see?

Excerpt 1: Conversation with Profe. Romilda, Escuela San Blás (10/22/2008). *This is the rural Guarani-dominant, economically disadvantaged school.*

I ask Profe. Romilda (kindergarten/1st grade teacher) how she uses Spanish and Guaraní in teaching. She says she uses Spanish for **aplicación** 'implementation or direct instruction' and Guaraní for **explicación** 'explanation'. **Lo que necesitan es el castellano porque ya dominan el guaraní** 'what they need is Spanish because they already speak Guaraní well.' They are all Guaraní speakers at home so she echoes Directora Felicita's opinion that they need Spanish at school. She says that teachers used to only speak Spanish to the students. Most of the students now can understand both Spanish and Guarani because their parents speak both. Usually the kids are not lost now. Occasionally there are one or two kids who only understand Guarani and so she will realize that, she says, and speak Guarani to them. **Pero después se van mejorando** 'but then they continue on improving'. She says she mostly uses Spanish. It is important (for the students and for someone in general) to speak both Spanish and Guarani, she says, **para comunicarse mejor con la gente** 'to communicate better with people'. From what she says it sounds like they are taught to read and write in Spanish.

What is their mother tongue, I ask? She responds, **castellano** 'Spanish'. And I pause and look at her, and I say but here at this school most of the kids speak Guarani at home. **Nos consideramos como una escuela hispanohablante** 'we consider ourselves a Spanish-speaker school'. But the kids themselves, I ask? *Si* **realmente haríamos como tenía que ser, haríamos la modalidad guaranihablante** 'if we would do it like it should be done, we would do the modality for Guarani speakers' because their mother tongue is Guarani, she says. **Pero siempre fue considerada modalidad hispanohablante la escuela** 'but the school was always considered [as implementing] the modality for Spanish speakers'.

She says **la gente todavía piensa que hablar el guaraní significa que seas ignorante. Dicen, no hablas el guaraní** *nde* **guarango** 'people still think that to speak Guarani means that you are ignorant. They say, don't speak Guarani *you* guarango.' I ask what guarango means. She says **que sos campesino, indio, inculto, indígena** 'that you are a peasant, an indian, uncultured, indigenous.' She then says, and what should it mean if you are **indígena** 'indigenous'? That doesn't mean you are **inculto** 'uncultured'. But she affirms that what people mean when they say this is that people are **inculto** 'uncultured/unrefined'. She says the people who say things like this are people in the Escuela San Blás community who have already learned Spanish and **dicen esto a sus niños** 'they say this to their children.' They are **intentando corregirles pero lo hacen mal** 'trying to correct them but they do it wrong.' They should correct the kids' Guarani rather than telling them not to speak it, she says. This happens with people who speak Spanish to their kids and so the kids speak Spanish better and they try to speak Guarani and they make mistakes, and then the parents make fun of them and call them guarango.

Excerpt 2: Conversation with Sr. Hugo, business owner, Capitán Antón (7/29/2008). *The urban Spanish-dominant, middle-class community.*

I stop in to a leather goods shop in town and talk for a while with Sr. Hugo, the owner. We talk about Obama's campaign for US president and the history of racial discrimination in the US. I ask whether there are other types of discrimination here. Yes, there is economic discrimination, he says. Language? I ask. No, **ahora no, antes sí. Se prohibía el guaraní** 'not now; before, yes. Guarani was prohibited. You couldn't speak it on TV. They would edit out the portions of the interview in Guarani. Now they go interview a campesino and they ask him questions in Spanish and he can't speak Spanish well, so he answers in Guarani and it's no problem. Only for the **extranjeros** 'foreigners' [who don't understand Guarani] who are watching. **Antes se prohibía [el guaraní] en las escuelas. Pero se habló en las casas. Había un solo guaraní** 'Before [Guarani] was prohibited in schools. But it was spoken in homes. There was only one Guarani'. The people from Asunción, **no hablaba mucho guaraní. Le decía guarango a los que hablaron guaraní** 'they didn't speak much Guarani. They said guarango to people who spoke Guarani.' I ask about the term and he says in the Spanish dictionary it says that it means **guaso** 'rude/crude.' I ask what that means. **Una persona maleducada** 'someone badly brought up', someone who says sexual things to someone, a woman, he explains. Do people say guarango/a now? I ask. **No, ahora no se usa. Los adolecentes hablan el guaraní tranquilamente. Hasta en la tele sale.** 'No, it's not used now. Teenagers speak Guarani without a worry. It's even on TV.' It's everywhere, he says.

Excerpt 3: Conversation with Profe. Sara, Escuela San Blás (6/11/2008). *This is the rural Guarani-dominant, economically disadvantaged school.*
The teachers and I go for coffee during recess. It's cold and drizzling, and Profe. Elena (5th/6th grade teacher) and Profe. Sara (4th grade teacher) and I make some coffee in the little kitchen. I ask Profe. Sara about her comment from yesterday about wanting the students to have **una identidad mas amplia** 'a broader identity.' She says many times we here in the ESB community **tenemos vergüenza de hablar guaraní, sentimos inferiores por hablar guaraní, la gente del centro dice guarango** 'we feel embarrassed of speaking Guarani, we feel inferior for speaking Guarani, people from town say guarango.' I ask about that word, guarango. People still say it, she says. Who? I ask. People from **el centro** 'town'. For example, when they go for a tournament to a school in town kids say things like that in the hallway about their students. I ask what it means, besides someone who speaks Guarani. She says it's not in a good sense, but in a bad sense. **Ellos dicen campesino. Por qué vamos a tener vergüenza por la sola razón de ser del campo, de una zona rural? Para que ellos no se sientan así, inferior, debemos usar guaraní en mas primeros lugares.** 'They say campesino [peasant]. Why should we be embarrassed for the sole reason of being from the countryside, from a rural area? So that they [our children] don't feel that way, inferior, we should use Guarani in more high-status positions.' This is what she means by an **identidad mas amplia** 'a bigger identity', a more equal identity, so they feel equal to the people in town.

Excerpt 4: Sixth grade classroom at Escuela Coronel Insfrán (3/25/2008). *This is the urban Spanish-dominant, middle-class school.*

At 8:30 am the teacher steps out of the classroom and comes back about half an hour later. While she is gone the students are supposed to be copying a sample personal letter from the board and writing their own. They quickly get distracted and talk to each other. They begin to get loud and up until now I have been sitting in the back, writing notes and observing, but they seem less than aware of me, or at least aware that I am not going to step into the teacher position, and they go ahead and talk to each other loudly, sometimes shouting across the room. I hear Roberto yell *nderasore* [slightly altered form of an offensive term in Guaraní] and Magalí yells back "**¡Roberto! ¡Tu boca!** 'Roberto! Your mouth!'" Then Roberto and Nelson turn around and say to me in English "Hello Teacher." They come over to me and Roberto says "*Mba'eichapa nderera* 'What is your name?'" Manuel turns around and says "**¿Cómo es tu nombre?** 'What is your name?'" [translating for me] and Roberto and Nelson yell at him to be quiet. I say I understand and I answer in Guaraní. They exclaim "Ahhh!" And Roberto seems to try to think of something else to ask me but they laugh and end up going back to their seats. My guess is that they were checking to see if I understand Guaraní, having realized that I was in the room when Roberto said the offensive term.

From where I sit, I hear Roberto talking to Nelson in Guaraní, so I go up and squat next to them and ask them about this. I ask if they often speak in Guaraní. Roberto answers, "**Sí, por supuesto, (como) soy Paraguayo** 'yes, of course, (since) I'm Paraguayan.'"

Excerpt 4: Conversation with María Regina, age 16, urban community member (1/5/2008).

María Regina [a friend's daughter] volunteered for an international medical mission and translated between doctors and patients. She translated not just from Spanish to English and back, but also into Guaraní. Many of the patients spoke mostly Guaraní. She was shocked at her classmates who also volunteered and who are Paraguayan but don't speak Guaraní. She says she thought, "**Cómo que no sabes nada del guaraní y sos Paraguaya?** 'How do you know nothing of Guaraní and you Paraguayan?'"

Excerpt 5: Teachers' professional development workshop on the environment, Escuela Coronel Insfrán (2/22/2008). *This is the urban Spanish-dominant, middle-class school.*

Much of the conversation is dominated by discussion of yellow fever and dengue fever [of which there have been outbreaks recently]. Miguel Angel, the representative from the municipal government who is leading the workshop, complains about the indiscriminate cutting of trees, deforestation, in the country. Mosquitoes live in trees, he says, and when all the trees are cut, they migrate; they come to [the nearby suburb where the yellow fever epidemic began]. He says, "**extranjeros vienen, no les importa** 'foreigners come, they don't care'". Someone says they're **Brasileros** 'Brazilians.' Teachers echo the complaint. Then Miguel Angel gives a long stretch of talk all in Guarani. I know something is happening, because he has only used isolated words and phrases in Guarani before (and after) this and very few of those even (mostly Guarani folk terms for illnesses). I lean over to ask Profe. Carla (6th grade teacher) what he said. She says after a minute, "**Nuestra gente no está haciendo la deforestación. Son extranjeros. Nuestra gente está acostumbrada a tener muchos arboles en su casa, plantar naranjos, colgar su hamaca entre dos arboles** 'Our people are not doing the deforestation. They are foreigners. Our people are accustomed to having many trees in their house, planting orange trees, hanging their hammock between two trees.'" So they wouldn't cut all the trees down, she explains.

Analyzing Together

Talk as a whole class. Looking at all five excerpts from Katherine's field notes, do you see examples of language ideologies? Give examples of ideologies about Guarani and about Spanish from this data. Do you see any contradictory ideologies here? If so, what are they?

Ideologies of Guarani	Ideologies of Spanish

Analyzing Together

Looking again at Katherine's five field note excerpts, what evidence do you see of ideologies about Guarani speakers? Spanish speakers? How do people define the term *guarango*?

Guarani Speakers	Spanish Speakers	Definitions of Guarango

When you start looking, ideologies are everywhere, aren't they? Katherine was asking people about how and where they used which language, and she learned a lot about what people's language ideologies were. But remember, her intention was to understand how those ideologies were connected to the policy change that happened in 1992, which required the use of and instruction in both Guarani and Spanish in schools. One way to do that is to look at actual policy documents, and that's certainly something she did. But policy isn't just in legal papers. Along with ideologies shaping and being shaped by our daily practices, they are also in our institutions. While accompanying the sixth graders from Escuela Coronel Insfán on a field trip, Katherine went to a museum called **La Casa de la Independencia** 'the House of Independence', and as always, she was on the lookout for ideologies. Here is an excerpt from her field notes concerning that visit:

Excerpt 6: A visit to La Casa de la Independencia, a museum in a house in downtown Asunción where the movement for liberation from Spain began (6/26/2008).
I ask the docent why there is no mention of Guarani in the whole museum. I say that I thought it was important to the Paraguayan identity. She says, oh yes, it is but this is a historical museum. You have to go to the ethnocultural museum to see the part about Guarani. I ask if the founding fathers spoke Guarani, and she says, yes, they all did. Did any of the documents that they produced have Guarani in them? No, she says, they were all in Spanish because the documents had to be sent to Spain. It was in the **cultura oral** 'oral culture,' she says, they didn't write it. She tells me that it was transmitted by mothers, and it was very important. "**Si hablás guaraní, ya sos Paraguayo** 'If you speak Guarani, you are already Paraguayan.'"

Interpreting Together

What do you think the absence of Guarani in the exhibit means? Katherine mentioned in her description of her study that language ideologies were complex and often contradictory. When you look at this piece of data in relation to the previous excerpts, do you see contradictory ideologies? If so, what are they?

Next you will see four of Katherine's interview excerpts. The first one is a group interview with sixth graders. It is long, and we will discuss this one right after you read it. The other three are from individual interviews. As you read, think about the ideologies, or beliefs about the world, and about the proper ways to use language that you see evidence for.

Excerpt 7: Group interview with several sixth graders (Group 4), Escuela San Blás (10/8/2008). *This is the rural, Guarani-speaking economically disadvantaged school.*

1	Ramón	Y yo también cuando suelo	And me too when I often
2		hablar con mi papá hablo en	speak with my father I speak in
3		guaraní me equivoco *eñe'ẽ*	Guarani I make mistakes *speak to*
4		*cheve castellanome nde*	*me in Spanish you*
5		*guarango* me dice	*guarango* he says ((all four students laugh))
6	KM	Qué te dice?	What does he say to you?
7		Qué te dice?	What does he say to you?
8	Ramón	Guarango. Porque no	Guarango. Because I don't
9		entiendo mucho guaraní	understand much Guarani
10	Deisy	Guaraní es del guarango	Guarani is of the guarango
11	KM	Qué quiere decir guarango?	What does guarango mean?
12	Ramón	Que hablaba mucho en	That I spoke a lot in
13		Guaraní	Guarani
14	Deisy	Guaraní	Guarani
15	Ramón	Yo guaraní utilizo poco	I use Guarani very little
16	KM	Entonces qué te dice sobre—	And so what does he say about— that
17		que vos sos guarango o que	you are guarango or that
18		no sos guarango	you're not guarango
19	Ramón	No cuando yo hablo en	No when I speak in
20		guaraní me dice guarango	Guarani he calls me guarango
21	KM	Ah— y eso— para— para decirte	Ah— and that— to— to tell you
22		Que	That
23	Ramón	Vamos a decir que no hablo en	Let's say that I don't speak in

24		mucho guaraní o que el	Guarani much or that
25		guaraní no entiendo mucho,	Guarani I don't understand much,
26		poco utilizo el guaraní	I use Guarani very little
27	KM	Entonces está burlándose de	And so he is making fun of
28		Vos	You
29	Ramón	Sí	Yes ((nods))
30	KM	Está burlándose de vos porque	He is making fun of you because
31		no hablas bien el guaraní?	you don't speak Guarani well?
32	Ramón	Sí	Yes ((nods and smiles))
33	KM	Entonces está diciendo que	And so he is saying that
34		no sos guarango verdad?	you are not guarango right?
35	Ramón	No	No
36	KM	Qué— qué es guarango?	What— what is guarango?
37	SS	Que hablas	That you speak
38		todo mal el guaraní	Guarani all wrong
39	KM	Hablar mal el guaraní	To speak Guarani wrong
40	Ramón	Hablar el guaraní te	Speaking Guarani you make mistakes
41		equivocás continuado	continuously
42		otra vez te equivocás otra vez	again you make mistakes again
43	KM	Aaa entonces no es que una	Aaa so it's not that a
44		persona que— una persona	person who— a person
45		habla mucho el guaraní. Es	speaks a lot of Guarani. It's
46		una persona que no habla	a person who doesn't speak

47		bien el guaraní	Guarani well
48	Deisy	Sí	Yes
49	KM	Así es?	That's how it is?
50	Yamil	Sí	Yes ((nods))
51	Ramón	Sí	Yes ((nods))
52	KM	Entonces él quiere que	And so he wants you to
53		hables bien el guaraní	speak Guarani well
54	Ramón	Sí, quiere que hable	Yes, he wants me to speak
55		bien hable bien el guaraní	well for me to speak Guarani well
56		quiere que practique en	he wants me to practice at
57		casa o acá.	home or here.

Analyzing Together

Think back to the chart you completed earlier in this chapter with a column about definitions of the term *guarango*. Now consider this new data. Is a coherent ideology about the term *guarango* emerging? If so, what is your evidence? Is it contradictory? If so, what is your evidence?

In the following three interview excerpts, think about national identity. Is speaking Guarani aligned to what it means to be Paraguayan? If so, how? If not, how?

Excerpt 8: Mother of Leticia, sixth grader, Escuela San Blás (9/3/2008). *This is the rural, Guarani-speaking economically disadvantaged school.*

1	Yo opino que está bien [que la	I think that it's good [that the
2	propuesta Ley de Lenguas manda	proposed Law of Languages mandate
3	que los funcionarios públicos	that public employees
4	puedan hablar] en guaraní porque	can speak] in Guarani because
5	acá todos somos Paraguayos y	here we are all Paraguayans and

6 ((se ríe)) está bien que hable en	((laughs)) it's good that one speaks in
7 guaraní-guaraní.	Guarani-Guarani.

Excerpt 9: Profe. Ninina, music teacher at Escuela Coronel Insfrán, also mother of Sofía, a sixth grader (5/26/2008). *This is the urban Spanish-speaking middle-class school.*

1 Así nos dice la constitución	That's what the constitution tells us
2 que es ambas lenguas son oficiales	that it is both languages are official
3 que conozcamos nuestro nuestra	that we [should] know our our
4 lengua conocer y valorar	language know and value the
5 la lengua y que se utiliza	language and that it is used
6 correctamente	correctly.

Excerpt 10: Mother of Yamil, sixth grader, Escuela Coronel Insfrán (7/28/2008). *This is the urban Spanish-speaking middle-class school.*

1 Nosotros mismos ese no hablamos	We ourselves eh don't speak
2 nuestro idioma el guaraní. Hay	our language Guarani. There are
3 muchas criaturas que no conoce	many children who don't know
4 el guaraní porque la mamá	Guarani because the mother
5 le prohíbe— que no	doesn't allow him— that she doesn't
6 quiere que hablar el guaraní . . . una	want him to speak Guarani . . . a
7 criatura de acá se va en el	child from here goes to the
8 asentamiento. *Nde reñe'ê la guarani*	squatters camp. *You speak Guarani*
9 pues le dice a mi hijo porque ellos	well, he says to my son because they
10 hablan pues y medio se burlan de	speak [it] and they kind of make fun
11 él. Y cómo como Paraguayo	of him. And how as a Paraguayan
12 le dice sos Paraguayo?	does he say you're Paraguayan?

Analyzing Together

Based on the last three interview excerpts you read, do you see a norm about how people talk about what it means to be Paraguayan? If so, what is it? Looking at the same data, are there resistances to that norm? If so, what are they?

Norms of National Identity	Resistances to the Norms of National Identity

---

Ideologies influence our daily practices both actively and passively. We may be fully conscious of some tenet of our belief system and choose to act the way we do because of our concern for performing in accord with that system. On the other hand, we may be unaware of certain principles that guide our practices but nevertheless perform in ways that fully correspond to those principles. Sometimes it is because the ethnographer has asked about a particular practice or belief that an ideology moves from unconscious awareness to conscious knowledge. Let's consider all of the data we've seen from Katherine's study.

Talking Together

As a whole class, identify the ideologies that Katherine's research suggests:

1. Guide the use of Spanish and Guarani in Paraguay;
2. Guide the attitudes toward the use of Spanish and Guarani in Paraguay; and
3. Guide the ideologies about speakers of Spanish and speakers of Guarani.

Van Dijk (1998) reminds us that "if we want to know what ideologies actually look like, how they work, and how they are created, changed and reproduced, we need to look closely at their *discursive manifestations*" (p. 6). Throughout this chapter, we have explored the discursive manifestations of ideologies, with a focus on ideologies of language and ideologies of the nation. Van Dijk doesn't want us to think about ideologies as being exactly the same as a 'worldview', though. Instead, he suggests that ideologies are the foundations for our worldviews. "Ideologies", he says, "thus operate both at the overall, global level of social structure, for instance as the socially shared mental 'monitor' of social competition, conflict, struggle and inequality, and at the local level of situated social practices in every-day life" (p. 8). We hope you are starting to see the ways in which understanding ideologies can help you begin to build your macro-level analysis of your data.

● ● ● ● ●

Nike Town

The fascinating and complex worlds of Paraguayan Guarani and Span-ish speakers may or may not be far away from your experience. We hope you are thinking about ideologies not just as things that people in other countries have but as things that shape and are shaped by your own daily practices. Ideologies can be visual as well as verbal. Consider Penaloza's (1998) study, "Just Doing It: A Visual Ethnographic Study of Spectacular Consumption Behavior at Nike Town". It is an ethno-graphic inquiry into ideologies that may be closer to home. It's also an example of a study in which the data involves photographs as well as interviews and participant observation. Her piece appeared in *Con-sumption, Markets and Culture* in 1998. The study was an exploration of the ways people consume spectacle at Nike Town in Chicago, which is a hybrid between a store and a museum. While you will benefit from reading the entire article, we have excerpted a passage below:

Data Record

The qualitative data that formed the basis of this study were col-lected via the ethnographic methods of participant observation and photography at Nike Town, supplemented with interviews with employees and consumers at the site, corporate documents, and ethnographic reflections of my experiences in and outside the store with sports and with Nike merchandise. The qualitative data record consisted of 148 pages of fieldnotes, 58 pages of journal entries, and 357 photographs from twenty-four hours of field obser-vation at the store. In addition, 98 pages of notes were compiled as I made coding sheets of descriptive and summary data from the pho-tographs. Artifacts included corporate annual reports, a nine page history of the company, 11 brochures, a series of advertisements, and a thick folder of newspaper clippings.

In the fieldnotes I sought detailed documentation of consum-ers' activities and the displays at the store. Participant observation activities included tracing my path through the store, with atten-tion to feelings and memories of past sports activities triggered by the design and displays, observing consumers, and documenting my participation with consumers and employees, soliciting their comments, reactions, and answers to specific questions.

Photographs were taken of all rooms and displays, and a sampling of consumers' and employees' activities. Photos were taken late mornings and afternoons, on weekdays and weekends. During low traffic times it was easier to observe consumers and document displays, and during high traffic times the photographs were less obtrusive. I used standard 50 mm, wide angle, and zoom lenses to provide detailed records of the agents, displays and artifacts. The wide angle lens provided good coverage of displays; the zoom lens provided close up detail, and the 50 mm lens standardized the size of persons and objects relative to the displays. Attention to figure/ ground contrast helped study depth and the shifting positionality and perspective of consumers moving through the site. I shifted the focus from figure to ground, and from consumers/displays in the foreground to consumers/displays in the background to recreate the depth of visual fields at the site.

Importantly, the photographs enabled written records of greater detail of what was viewed at the time and described in fieldnotes. Their subsequent viewing provided additional information regarding consumers' activities and physical characteristics. In drawing data from the photographs, I first made impressionistic notes of their contents, and then developed detailed coding sheets. Each photograph was numbered, and its location and the types of social groups and interactions were listed. Socio-demographics, activities, positions and focal points were then detailed for each discernible individual. Given the visual nature of the data, the codings should be viewed with attention to the range of employees' and consumers' characteristics and activities, rather than their statistically representative occurrence.

Unstructured interviews were used to dialogue with consumers and employees regarding findings and interpretive themes derived primarily from the visual data, in reversal of their customary role as primary data. Pseudonyms were used for consumers and employees to maintain their anonymity and confidentiality, although employees were most vulnerable due to job concerns. Of interviews with 26 consumers in the store, fourteen were male and twelve female. Regarding race/ethnicity, three were African American, four were Latino and eighteen were White. Customers were asked how they had heard about the store, whether they had been here before, their reactions, what they liked best, and whether they had bought anything. I approached most of the consumers, although some contacts were initiated by consumers interested in my activities taking notes and pictures.

Twenty-two employees were interviewed. Ten were women, twelve were men; and three were Latino, five were African American, three were Asian and 11 were White. Five were managers, while 17 were sales associates. Employees were asked how long they had worked here and which celebrities they had seen as icebreakers.

Additional questions included what their experiences had been here, what kind of training they had received, the questions they were most frequently asked by consumers, how they were paid, and their sales record. As with consumers, employees' questions regarding what I was doing gave me the opportunity to dialogue with them.

Finally, comparative site visits were made to the Nike Town in Orange County, California in 1995 and 1996. One hundred photographs and 33 pages of fieldnotes were compiled from the field visits. Of interest were similarities and differences between the two field sites in their design, displays, and consumer and employee characteristics and activities.

Looking Together

We want you to think about Penaloza's study because the ideologies aren't necessarily embedded in utterances. Her analysis combines talk about Nike Town, field notes from participant observation, and images.

1. What kinds of ethnographic data did Penaloza collect?

2. Summarize Penaloza's discussion regarding how the design of her study emerged over time.

3. Penaloza focuses her study on what she terms 'spectacular consumption'. What does she mean by that? Explain 'spectacular consumption' in your own words.

4. How do Penazola's field notes, interviews, and photographs work together to contribute to her interpretation of Nike Town?

5. Penaloza identifies the cultural meanings or ideologies she recognizes as underlying consumption behavior at Nike Town. List all of those ideologies below and, for each, also provide a short summary of how that ideology is manifested.

	Ideologies	How They Were Manifested
1		
2		
3		

● ● ● ● ●

Building Your Ethnographic Analysis

As we end this chapter, it's time for you to again return to your own data. What are the ideologies you see there? Do you have examples of ideologies in talk? In your field notes? In photographs? Make a three-column list here. In the left column, list the ideologies you have identified in your data. In the middle column, write where you have found them (interviews, field notes, artifacts, photographs, or video-recordings). In the third column, write down some examples of the evidence for these ideologies. Are there connections among your three columns? What might the connections be?

Looking at My Data

Ideologies	Where I Found Them	Evidence From My Data

● ● ● ● ●

Wrapping Up

In this chapter, we identified and tried to understand ideologies that underlie the practices in our ethnographic data. With examples of ideologies that dealt with language and the nation, and with multiple modalities, we attempted to help you start thinking about the connections between ideologies and macro-level analysis. Now you have experience looking for ideologies in other people's data. We hope that practice will help you to start looking for ideologies in your own data. Who knows what you will find!

This article and others that appear in various chapters as examples of ethnographic inquiry can be accessed through your university library, and the information you need to search for them is available in the References section at the end of this chapter:

● ● ● ● ●

References

Hammersley, M., & Atkinson, P. (2007). *Ethnography: Principles in practice* (3rd ed.). London: Routledge.

Mortimer, K. S. (2012). *The Guarani speaker in Paraguayan bilingual education policy: Language policy as metapragmatic discourse.* Unpublished PhD dissertation: University of Pennsylvania.

Penaloza, L. (1998). Just doing it: A visual ethnographic study of spectacular consumption behavior at Nike Town. *Consumption, Markets and Culture, 2*(4), 337–400.

Van Dijk, T. A. (1998). *Ideology: A multidisciplinary approach.* London: Sage.

10

•••••

Review With Participants

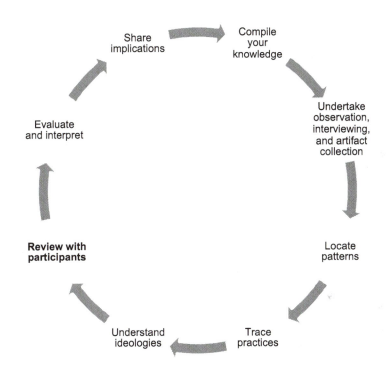

Share implications → Compile your knowledge → Undertake observation, interviewing, and artifact collection → Locate patterns → Trace practices → Understand ideologies → Review with participants → Evaluate and interpret →

When we consider the next step in our CULTURES framework—Review With Participants—we are thinking about how we can check what we think we have learned with the people we have worked with in our study. Is our data trustworthy? Did we understand what they told us? Did we interpret our data in a way that makes sense to the participants? Of course, there will be multiple perspectives when it comes to this. Some people may agree, and others may not. That's part of the messiness of qualitative research. This chapter looks at the process of conducting member checks in your communities of practice, and it also discusses how you might share your findings with the community you worked with in ways that will make sense to them.

Member checks mean checking with the people in your study to make sure you understood them. Sometimes member checks are done individually; sometimes they are done in groups. It depends. Usually the researcher writes up a summary or a transcript of interviews that have been conducted with a person or a group or, preferably, both. Of course, the language that the participants are most comfortable with is the language you should use. Sometimes member checks involve asking participants to read your summary of the data. Other times, you read the data to the participants, and a conversation about the particulars ensues. Some researchers make a decision to share only the data that is specific to a person with that individual. Other researchers choose to share summaries of individual data, along with the overall data from the entire study (protecting confidentiality, of course).

Lincoln and Guba (1985) explain:

> *The member check, whereby data, analytic categories, interpretations, and conclusions are tested with members of those stakeholding groups from whom the data were originally collected is the most crucial technique for establishing credibility. . . . Member checking is both informal and formal, and it occurs continuously. Many opportunities for member checks arise daily in the course of the investigation.*
>
> *(p. 314)*

These are important points: member checking is both formal and informal, and it is continuous. That is, you do it again and again, throughout the course of your study.

● ● ● ● ●

Kinds of Member Checks

Based on our experiences in the field, we think of there being two levels of member checks. One involves checking the accuracy of what you heard and saw, **checking the data**. The other is about asking participants to review your **interpretation of the data**. This technique can be quite powerful, but it depends on who your participants are. Sometimes it's not appropriate to share your interpretations with the people in your study. What do we mean by that? Well, first of all, if you are working with young children, people with disabilities, and/or people with little formal education, it can be difficult to engage them in your analysis. But you should still try to do it.

Other times, sharing your interpretation of the whole study could compromise the confidentiality of other participants. That is, even though you're using pseudonyms, it's still possible for people's identities to be revealed, especially in a small community. In that situation, it's probably best to do individual member checks.

But most of the time, sharing your interpretations of the study along with summaries of the data can be important in developing the trustworthiness of your study (Maxwell, 2010). Triangulation is another vital aspect of establishing trustworthiness, as mentioned throughout this book. It relies on three data-gathering methods to solidify your study. Getting data from interviews, participant observation, and artifacts helps to make sure you're getting a holistic picture of a community.

Formal Member Checks

In an ethnography of communication study, the formal member check, the step of reviewing your data with participants in a detailed way, is something that happens before you share your study with scholarly communities. It is a way of checking the trustworthiness of the data you have collected, and you do it before you write up the final or close-to-final versions of your study.

For instance, when Char did a series of formal member checks with undocumented participants in one of her studies, she was at the stage of having just begun to sit down with her data. She was getting familiar with the huge amount of data she had collected, and she was reading and reading, a process you have gotten a taste of in Chapters 7, 8, and 9. That was a good time for her to return to the study participants to see what they thought about her data.

She wrote up a summary of the things she had learned from each person in the study, along with an overview of all the data she had gathered, with people's identities protected, of course. The people she worked with didn't want to read what she had, but they were happy for her to read it to them and to talk about it afterwards. The part of what she had learned that stood out overwhelmingly to the participants was the exhaustive list of all the unjust and downright horrendous practices that employers had used with undocumented employees. Even the individual summaries were overwhelming. When the participants were confronted with the collective injustices that their community had experienced, several of the people in her study said they didn't want to tell such a depressing story to the world. They wanted people to think of them as successful, in spite of their difficult situations. After more conversation, Char asked them whether the things she had read to them were accurate. They agreed they were. Then they talked about what it might mean for people to learn about these shameful employment practices. Several participants said that maybe there would be more support for immigration reform if *los güeros* (White people) knew what really happened to undocumented people. As Char presented the summaries of her findings, listening and staying out of the conversation, slowly people came to a group consensus that her findings were accurate and that she should move forward. But there were tense moments. She didn't want to convince anyone of anything, and, fortunately, she wasn't in that situation. Char conducted member checks with six groups of participants for that study, and each of the member check groups decided that they were comfortable with what she had found. But the conversation about whether or not they should air their dirty laundry came up with every member check group. Even though we use pseudonyms, people still have the right to control what is said about them. This step in the CULTURES process isn't just about ensuring the trustworthiness of the data we have collected. It's also about consulting with the people in our studies and giving them a chance to discuss the project and its implications for them.

Collaborative Ethnography

Ethnographers must rely greatly on the participants they have observed and interviewed throughout their research. Having a participant to talk with and ask questions of provides you with a guide to understanding what you have observed and learned. Study participants can help ethnographers identify the meaningful practices in the data, or sometimes their own ideologies and interpretation of it are discussed, all depending on the situation.

Char has a friend who studied some social justice–oriented nonprofit groups, and the members were highly educated and interested in her study. They wanted to be part of the interpretation of the data. In some ways, they collaborated with the researcher.

There are theorists who talk about participants collaborating on the analysis of the study or even becoming co-investigators. According to Rappaport (2008), collaborative ethnography can make a significant contribution both in its product—an explanation of a community—and in its existence as a "space for the coproduction of theory, which is . . . a crucial venue in which knowledge is created through collaboration" (p. 1).

Collaboration in ethnographic analysis takes place throughout the processes of observation and analysis. In the context of our CULTURES model, collaboration should be active within each step of the cycle. What might that look like? Soon after being a participant observer at a community event, or conducting an interview, the researcher reviews field notes and interview content with select participants. Often this is done informally, and it becomes a conversation. Member checking is also done more formally, usually in the data analysis phase.

As we noted earlier, interviewing members of the community within which we are participating and observing is one example of a collaborative endeavor that marks ethnographic fieldwork. We must also recognize that collaboration is essential as the researcher draws near to the final analysis and writing up of results. It is at this stage in the model, then, that we call on collaboration again—most consciously and formally—provide us with explanation, deeper understanding, and, perhaps, correction of what we believe we have learned and what we now (think we) know about the community.

● ● ● ● ●

The Complexities of Member Checks

While reviewing with participants is important to the ethnographic process, it presents issues of its own in terms of the credibility it lends our analysis. Citing Morse (1994), Angen (2000), and Sandelowski (1993), Cohen and Crabtree (2006) provide a list of positive and negative aspects of member checks. The mixed bag that is the member check can include the following:

- Different members may have different views of the same data.
- Participants have the opportunity to correct errors and challenge what are perceived as wrong interpretations.
- Respondents may disagree with the researcher's interpretations. Then the question of whose interpretation should stand becomes an issue.
- Members may not be in the best position to check the data. They may forget what they said or the manner in which a story was told.
- Members may participate in checking only to be 'good' respondents and agree with an account in order to please the researcher.
- Participants can add information that may grow from the member check process.
- Member checking can depend on the problematic assumption that there is a fixed reality that can be accounted for by a researcher and confirmed by a respondent.
- Both researchers and members are stakeholders in the research process and have different stories to tell and agendas to promote. This can result in conflicting ways of seeing interpretations.
- Researchers come to understand and assess what participants intended to do through their actions.
- Members strive to be perceived as good people; researchers strive to be seen as good scholars. These divergent goals may shape findings and result in different ways of seeing and reacting to data.

■ Members may tell stories during an interview that they later regret or see differently. Members may deny such stories and want them removed from the data.

You can see that many complex issues can arise when conducting member checks. At the same time, they can be beneficial to the trustworthiness of your study. The reality is that ethnographic research can be messy. You have to be willing to live with that messiness.

Talking Together

Work in small groups. Talk about the influence of each of the aspects in the list above on your research process, your data, and your findings up to this point. As you talk with one another, identify those aspects you view as beneficial to your study and those aspects with which you need to be cautious.

View as Beneficial	Use Cautiously

Share your group's chart with the whole class. Do you have different opinions about each complexity of member checking? Explain your thoughts.

Thinking Together

Read Julie Carlson's (2010) advice about integrating member checks into a research project in her article at http://files.eric.ed.gov/fulltext/EJ896214.pdf. Pay special attention to the descriptions of member checks she had conducted and then to the advice she provides.

Now, consider this question with your classmates: Given the cautions that must be incorporated into the use of member checks, are they worth the effort? Why or why not?

While member checks will help you at each stage of the ethnographic process, they are also important as you complete your research. We have placed this component of the process near the end of our CULTURES mnemonic to remind us that before we are ready to contemplate and share the results of our research, we must ensure that we have spoken with our participants at least one more time to gather any knowledge our participants may have about their community or our project. It is an opportunity for you to ask lingering questions, and it is a chance for the participants to reflect on what will be communicated in your study.

Ethnographic research is a recursive process. Throughout the stages of data collection and analysis, recursivity allows for review, reconsideration, and revision of hypotheses and conclusions (LeCompte, 1999). Throughout all stages of the inquiry—from initial contact with community members through drafting of the final report—data gained throughout the research process by way of participant observation, interviewing, and artifact collection is continually written up and examined for patterns and their meanings. With recursivity, neither note taking nor analysis, and neither interviewing nor coding, is limited to a moment in time but is extended over time as the ethnographer continually integrates insights.

● ● ● ● ●
Playback

Along with conducting member checks, ethnographers of communication can adopt a technique called 'playback' from discourse analysts. Playback is defined by Roy (1999) as "interviews [that] allow an analyst to replay an interaction for the participants (on an individual basis) and ask for their recollection of what they were thinking and their impressions of meanings. Obviously, these interviews need to be conducted soon after the original event before participants' memories fade away" (p. 50). We recommend that this occur no more than two weeks after the initial interaction. Playback is traditionally undertaken with audio- or video-recordings of observations and/or interviews; however, you may use your written notes for playback as well. As you review your data with your participants, ask them to tell you when they come to a portion that they wish to comment on. Give them agency and ownership of some of the analysis and of their contributions to your study.

The process for engaging a participant in playback is meant to gain open-ended responses to the data you have collected from one or more of the individuals you have observed or interviewed. Explain playback to your participants as an opportunity for you to sit with them while you both go through your data—notes and/or tapes.

● ● ● ● ●
Sharing Your Findings With Your Community of Practice

Conducting member checks isn't the same as sharing the final results of your study with the people who participated in your study. Many times, the academic journal to which you plan to submit your manuscript will not be read by your participants. How might you re-imagine a way to present your findings to the study participants that will be accessible to them? LeCompte and Schensul (2010) suggest transforming your data into performances, spoken-word poetry, videos, *fotonovelas*, even dances. They encourage you to organize an event at which participants feel welcomed and comfortable.

Thinking Together

Work in a small group. How will you share your study findings with the participants in your study? LeCompte and Schensul (2010) suggest you think about sharing your results with the community of practice by considering the factors below.

What formats?	
By whom?	
Where?	
How?	

●●●●●
Other Contexts for Member Checks

As we have done in previous chapters, let's read an ethnographic analysis that illustrates our chapter focus. In "Learning to Love Yourself: Esthetics, Health, and Therapeutics in Brazilian Plastic Surgery", Alexander Edmonds (2009) examines the phenomenon he labels 'esthetic health', which he defines as "the 'union' of reconstructive and cosmetic procedures ... that ... operate not on pathologies or defects, but on a suffering psyche" (p. 466).

Thinking Together

While reading "Learning to Love Yourself", take note of the sources of Edmonds' data. In particular, keep track of the information he obtains from interviewing. Create a chart like the one below to complete as you read.

Participant Interviewed	Information Shared

After completing the chart, identify the common content that different participants shared. Talk with your classmates about how Edwards uses these patterns to make the conclusions he does about how the physical and psychological are both addressed in plastic surgery.

●●●●●

Building Your Ethnographic Analysis

As we end this chapter, it's time for you to again return to your own data. Have you been conducting informal member checks? It's likely that you have. When will you plan to conduct a more formal member check? It's probably time to think about that. How will you approach it? Will you try the playback technique? Will you do individual member checks? Group member checks? Both? And after you have completed your study, how will you share your findings with the community of practice? How will you translate and transform your academic study into something more accessible and useful for the community? Complete this chart to help you start thinking about member checking and sharing your findings.

Looking at My Data

Approaches to Member Checking	Plan for When to Conduct a Formal Member Check	Ideas About How to Share My Findings

●●●●●

Wrapping Up

In this chapter, we looked at the complex and important issues involved in conducting member checks, or reviewing your data and interpretation with participants. We presented a variety of approaches for you to consider using. We also encouraged you to think about how you might translate your study findings into a form that would make sense for the participants in your study, especially if they don't read academic journals.

This article and others that appear in various chapters as examples of ethnographic inquiry can be accessed through your university library, and the information you need to search for them is available in the References section at the end of this chapter:

●●●●●

References

Angen, M. J. (2000). Evaluating interpretive inquiry: Reviewing the validity debate and opening the dialogue. *Qualitative Health Research*, 10(3), 378–395.

Carlson, J. A. (2010). Avoiding traps in member checking. *The Qualitative Report*, 15(5), 1102–1113. Retrieved from http://www.nova.edu/ssss/QR/QR15-5/carlson.pdf

Cohen, D., & Crabtree, B. (2006). Qualitative research guidelines project. Retrieved from http://www.qualres.org/HomeMemb-396.html

Edmonds, A. (2009). Learning to love yourself: Esthetics, health, and therapeutics in Brazilian plastic surgery. *Ethnos, 74*(4), 465–489.

LeCompte, M. D. (1999). *Analyzing and interpreting ethnographic data.* Walnut Creek, CA: Altamira.

LeCompte, M. D., & Schensul, J. J. (2010). *Designing and conducting ethnographic research.* Vol. 1. Walnut Creek, CA: Rowman Altamira.

Lincoln, Y. S., & Guba, E. G. (1985). *Naturalistic inquiry.* Newbury Park, CA: Sage.

Maxwell, J. A. (2010). Validity: How might this be wrong? In Luttrell, W. (Ed.), *Qualitative educational research: Readings in reflexive methodology and transformative practice* (pp. 279–287). New York: Routledge.

Morse, J. (1994). Designing funded qualitative research. In Denzin, N. K., and Lincoln, Y. S. (Eds.), *Handbook of qualitative research* (pp. 220–235). Thousand Oaks, CA: Sage.

Rappaport, J. (2008). Beyond participant observation: Collaborative ethnography as theoretical innovation. *Collaborative Anthropologies, 1*, 1–31.

Roy, C. B. (1999). *Interpreting as a discourse process.* New York: Oxford University Press.

Sandelowski, M. (1993). Rigor or rigor mortis: The problem of rigor in qualitative research revisited. *Advances in Nursing Science, 16*(2), 1–8.

11

•••••

Evaluate and Interpret

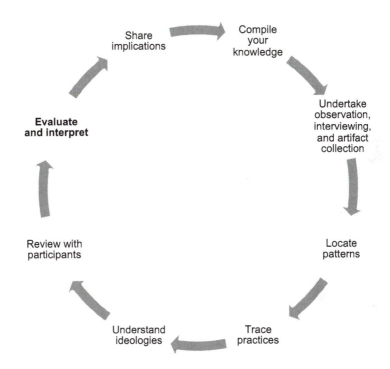

How do you go from having found patterns and themes in your data to creating an entire analysis? And then how does that analysis become a final paper for your class and/or a manuscript to submit to a scholarly journal? Evaluating and interpreting your data, or data analysis, is a process of making sense. If your study is appropriately doable, you will still have a lot of data to reckon with. Also, it's important to know that writing up your ethnography of communication study is a rhetorical practice. That is, you interpret your data in relation to theory, and you make a persuasive argument about what your data means. In this chapter, we present the ways we think it makes sense to approach data analysis and writing in the ethnography of communication study. As you conduct more research, you may find there are other ways that work for you. That's OK. The actual process of evaluating and interpreting ethnography of communication data has been rather individual, and as Char's mother used to say about things that were unknown, it was "lost in the mists of antiquity". Although there are many ways to evaluate and interpret your data, as well as to write it up, we offer some fairly simple guidelines about how to systematically analyze your data and to prepare it for a scholarly audience.

●●●●●
Where Do I Start?

Human behavior is messy. Do you remember our saying that early on? Well, it should feel experientially true right now. This is the moment in the CULTURES process in which you sit down with all of the data you have collected, organize it, and interpret it. Here are some of the kinds of data you *may* have at this point in your research process:

■ Participant observation field notes
■ Transcripts of audio-recorded interviews
■ Transcripts of audio- or video-recorded focus groups
■ Transcripts of audio- or video-recorded events
■ Electronic sources (e.g., Facebook pages, emails, listserv postings, texts, websites, MP3s)
■ Photographs, sketches, researcher-drawn maps
■ Documents (e.g., mission statements, policies, letters, school assignments, drawings, journals, advertisements)
■ Artifacts (e.g., jewelry, clothes, tattoos, cars, books)
■ _____ (fill in the blank)

Now it's time for you to interact with your data. You will read it again, and again, and again. And then you'll read it again. Think about the *how* of what people say and do, the *what* of what people say and do, and the *why* of what people say and do. This part of the process involves looking carefully at your data on the micro-level, the mid-level, and the macro-level of analysis. We suggest you look at the mid-level of analysis first, and that means identifying themes. We know it seems like we should go from micro-level to mid-level to macro-level analysis. However, the reason we suggest you start with themes is that the *what* of what people say is the most accessible to most of us. From there, we can look carefully at the *how* of language use, and ultimately combine both the *how* and the *what*, along with returning to the reading of social theory, to get us to ideas about the *why* of our data.

This is an excerpt from Char's *Inglés sin Barreras* (Ullman 2014) study that you saw in Chapter 7, where we used it to talk about transcription conventions. Now, let's look at it again and identify some themes. This is the excerpt Char had trouble understanding before she started reading new kinds of social theory. What themes do you see?

Excerpt 1: Magdelena

1	No me gustaría que se me pase la vida.	I don't want my life to pass by.
2	Si estoy viviendo en este país	If I am living in this country
3	y después siento que es una responsabilidad	and after, I feel a responsibility
4	aprender el ingles.	to learn English.
5	Para ser una mejor ciudadana.	To be a better citizen
6	Para, porque no he perdido las esperanzas	Because, I haven't lost hope
7	en un futuro	for the future
8	estudiar algo y prepararme.	to study something
9	Siento que sería un desperdicio	I feel like it would be a waste
10	hacerme vieja en la cocina,	for me to get old in the kitchen
11	cocinando	cooking
12	aprendiendo nada más de cocina	learning nothing more than cooking
13	y como llevar una casa).	and how to keep house.
14	TENGO QUE aprender.	I NEED to learn
15	Cuando Dios nos dió cerebro	God gave us a brain.
16	Y lo, pudo aprender algo más	And I can learn something more.
17	Y aporta	And to contribute
18	MI granito de arena	MY grain of sand
19	para la sociedad.	for society.

What themes did you identify? One might be *citizenship*. Magdalena talked about having the responsibility to learn English and about becoming a better citizen. She also talked about *education*. She said that she hoped to study something and that her brain must be for something, since God gave it to her. She spoke intensely about her need to learn. This seems like a major theme. And another theme that might be lurking here is that of *gender*. Magdalena seemed to say that doing the things housewives do (cooking and cleaning) isn't enough for her. She wanted to get an education as well. Perhaps gender and education are linked themes. Another subtler theme might be *finding meaning in life as one ages*. That is, Magdalena noted it would be a waste if she remained a housewife and didn't learn other things. She also said she wanted to contribute to society.

So some possible themes are:

- Citizenship
- Education, school, learning
- Gender
- Gender and education
- Finding meaning in life, contributing to society

The next step would be to go through that same process with all of your data. You may end up with more than a hundred themes, and at this point, it's OK. After you have gone through your data multiple times, you might find that some themes can be merged or that some individual themes are similar enough to each other to be considered a single theme. In this example, gender and education are good candidates for merging. You might find that some of the themes are too specific, or don't come up much. You may also find that some themes are more common in your data than others. Make a list of those. Evaluating and interpreting your data is not done in a day. Take your time and let the data speak to you.

It's best to have four to six themes that you can theorize about carefully, rather than a hundred among which are some that are almost the same and overlapping. Revise your themes until you have a group of them that it makes sense for you to focus on. Many people use programs such as NVivo to organize their data around themes. NVivo won't find the themes for you, but it is a useful organizing tool. Now, Char is using Transana to transcribe and analyze her data. She likes this program because it is based on audio- and video-recorded data, not on texts. If you are looking for themes that are words or phrases (such as some of the examples above), using the 'find' command in Microsoft Word or Mac Pages can be useful as well. Remember that last theme we identified, "finding meaning in life as one ages"? That is the kind of theme that can't be identified by a single word, so you would have to make sure you don't miss those subtler themes if you were to search for specific words. Marilyn Lichtman (2013) recommends using the comment function in Word to identify and keep track of themes as you read your data, and we think that is a great idea. If you do that, you can then search through the document for your themes. Finding themes is a way of categorizing your data. Many times we categorize things by what they have in common. Other times we categorize by difference.

Categorizing Together

Each student will bring five artifacts of any kind to class. They can be articles, books, images, websites, etc. They can be in any language or any genre.

Work in small groups. Look through the artifacts your group has. How could you categorize them? Come up with at least five ways to categorize them. Now, evaluate them. Which are the best ways? Why?

Categories	Evaluation (on a scale of 1–5; 5 is best)	Why It's Good

*Adapted from the work of Marilyn Lichtman (2013).

From here it makes sense to do micro-level analysis, looking at the *how* of what people say. Do you see patterns of language use within each theme? Within a speaker's utterances? Within a certain group of speakers? Judy's data about the salesperson–customer interactions demonstrated that salespeople were more likely to initiate greetings ("good morning") than customers were. Focus on the *how* of what people say. If you have video data, you might see repeated patterns of behavior there as well. Include all of it as you look for patterns. You may also find yourself seeing norms arise from that micro-level data analysis. That's important for you to note and explore as well. Even if you have only a small amount of data, you can pursue micro-analysis. But if for some reason you were not able to record your data, then you should not try do micro-analysis, because you dont' know the details of what people said. In that case, you should do mid-level and macro-level analysis.

The final level of analysis we encourage you to engage in is macro-level analysis. What do the practices and ideologies you have identified and organized mean? While you identify themes, it's likely that some of what you see will connect with theories you have read before. And as you find patterns at the micro-level of analysis, you may notice the ways people use language to distance themselves from an idea or align themselves with it. But it's also possible that your data won't have a connection to theoretical ideas that you know about. That's not bad. It's actually exciting. You need to keep reading and thinking about how to understand your data. Read current scholarly journals. Read theory. Researchers often go to conferences to learn about new approaches and to talk about data they don't yet understand.

● ● ● ● ●

The Dangers of Cherry-Picking

We always want data to lead the way when we do an analysis. That is, the social theories you have read shouldn't drive the data you collect. And you shouldn't ignore the majority of your data to follow one part that fits a theory you like. That's called cherry-picking—only considering the data that fits your theory. Most of the time, you will see patterns in your data, as well as themes, and you will be able to connect them to social theories. But sometimes you will see patterns that are equally strong, and perhaps even contradictory. That is a finding as well. Oftentimes, the journals that publish qualitative studies know that this can happen. It's important to be forthcoming about contradictory findings and to explore what they might mean.

Perhaps at this point you are feeling "lost in the mists of antiquity". We hope not. You may decide to connect your micro-level and macro-level data in your paper or manuscript. You might analyze your data at the mid- and macro-levels only. Or you might include micro-level, mid-level, and macro-level analysis in the final product of your ethnography of communication study. You are forming an argument about how readers should think about something, and you are using your data to support that argument.

● ● ● ● ●

How Do I Structure My Writing?

You may be tired of hearing this, but there is no set way that everyone agrees on to write an ethnography of communication study. However, there are components that are almost always present. They include:

■ An introduction;
■ A description of the context of the study;
■ A discussion about your positionality;
■ A look at other studies that have explored your topic;
■ Theory that explains your data interpretation;

- Your methods;
- Presentation of your data that has been analyzed with theory inter-woven; and
- A conclusion.

Your final product may include headings such as "introduction", "methods", and "conclusion". But the other headings should be your own. And there may be some movement in the order of the theory, the methods, and the other studies you have looked at, but the data analysis directly precedes the conclusion. In the section in which you discuss the data and connect it with theory, you may decide to use themes, descriptions of patterns, or quotations as headings. It's also common for ethnographers of communication to include vignettes, especially at the beginning of a manuscript, to capture the readers' attention. As we said early in this chapter, writing an ethnography of communication study is a rhetorical act.

Details of Ethnographic Writing

While you may have learned that all scholarly writing is written in the third person to lend it authority (i.e., "The results obtained included . . ."), in an ethnography of communication study, we prefer the first person, or the "I" form. You were there, and you were part of how the knowledge was produced. There's no need to pretend you were invisible. If you look at current scholarly journals, you will find that Judy and Char are not the only ones who feel this way.

Another detail of ethnographic writing is to avoid what is called "the ethnographic present". What that means is that you don't want to use narrative tools that leave the people in your study locked in the present tense. You exist in time just as they do. Even though your field notes are probably written in the present tense, because you were recording things that happened in the present, you need to translate actions and observations into the past tense when you write your final analysis.

Ethnographic writing also highlights interview data and includes excerpts of people's utterances that they produced in their interviews or as you observed their natural practice that you will analyze. The best ethnographic writing makes the participants' voices come alive. It also makes the context come alive. The way you bring in the context is by using thick description. Thick description is detailed writing about what you saw and heard in the field. It's also description that gives your reader context. You might write about the layout of the space you are in, the objects there, and of course the people—what they look like, what they are wearing, and the social relationships among them.

Anthropologist Clifford Geertz (1973) is the originator of the term "thick description", and he drew on the work of philosopher of language Gilbert Ryle to develop it. What does a wink mean? Well, it depends on the context. It could mean flirtation, it could be a way to communicate something particular, it could be a twitch . . . it depends on the context. The point of thick description is to show and not just tell.

Observing Together

Work with a partner. Look around your classroom. Each of you will write a thick description of your class. Describe the physical space and the objects in it, the people, what they look like, their relationships to each other, what the norms of the context are, and what the group is doing. How do people interact? What are their emotional states?

Read your thick description to your partner. Compare and contrast your examples of thick description. Are there things one person noticed that the other one didn't?

●　●　●　●　●

Multiple Audiences

And, finally, writing a paper for your instructor or a manuscript for a scholarly journal does not limit you to one audience. We all also have an obligation to share the results of our studies with the people who so generously shared their time with us and allowed us to participate in their communities.

Sometimes the participants in our studies will read our published work. That's great when it happens. But many times the participants in our studies don't read scholarly journals. If that's the case for your participants, then it makes sense for you to think about how you might communicate your findings to them. What do you think would be an appropriate way to share what you have found? In previous chapters, we have mentioned performances. How might you turn your results into a theatrical performance? Are there other ways you might approach sharing your findings? Be creative.

●　●　●　●　●

Building Your Ethnographic Analysis

As we end this chapter, it's time for you to again return to your own project. What are the findings of your study? How are you going to write it up? Fill in this chart and then discuss your plans with a partner.

Looking at My Data

Key Points of Analysis	*Writing Structure*

● ● ● ● ●

Wrapping Up

In this chapter, we have looked at how you can evaluate and interpret your data. This stage of the CULTURES process deals with interpreting your data and writing it up for your instructor and/or a scholarly journal. In the final chapter of this book, we will talk about how you decide which journal to send your manuscript to, and we will close by exploring the issues involved in academic publishing.

This article and others that appear in various chapters as examples of ethnographic inquiry can be accessed through your university library, and the information you need to search for them is available in the References section at the end of this chapter:

● ● ● ● ●

References

Geertz, C. (1973). *The interpretation of cultures: Selected essays.* New York: Basic Books.

Lichtman, M. (2013). *Qualitative research in education: A user's guide* (3rd ed.). Thousand Oaks, CA: Sage.

12
●●●●●

Share Implications

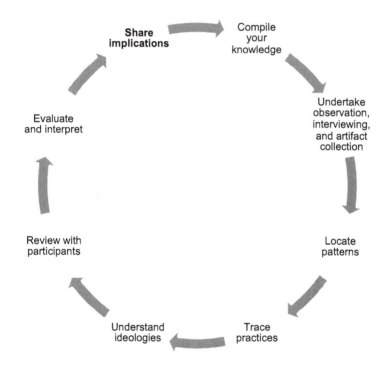

You shared the findings of your research with your community of practice in Chapter 11, both to do a member check and to communicate what you learned. We hope that your research will be helpful for the people with whom you worked, and that it may also contribute to positive social change.

But your work will also contribute to scholarly knowledge. You should share your research outside the community by presenting your findings at professional academic conferences and publishing your work in academic journals, conference proceedings, and edited volumes. That may sound intimidating, but this chapter will help you unravel the world of academic publishing.

● ● ● ● ●
Where Do I Begin?

If you feel scared about doing this, that's natural. It's a big deal to go from talking to the people you worked with, your classmates, and your professor and then . . . the world. Well, maybe it's not the world, but it is a larger academic discipline. The first thing you need to do is think about your audience. Because work that uses the ethnography of communication approach may be very inter-disciplinary, you need to think about how your work might fit in with different disciplines.

● ● ● ● ●
Getting Feedback at a Conference

Begin by selecting a discipline. Is your study speaking to people who care about a particular topic? Business? Communication? Health care? Education? Does it seem to fit into linguistics? Anthropology? Sociology? After you've determined what field makes sense for you, then you will look for scholarly conferences. Timing is everything when it comes to conferences. You usually need to send your proposal in six to eight months before the conference actually happens. Most conferences are in different cities every year. One way to find out about scholarly conferences is to talk with your professors and your classmates. It's also good to look at the websites for the professional organizations, societies, and associations that sponsor conferences. Here are some for you to consider:

	Scholarly Organization	Website
1	American Anthropological Association	aaanet.org
2	American Association of Applied Linguistics	aaal.org
3	American Educational Research Association	aera.net
4	American Sociological Association	asa.org
5	National Council of Teachers of English	ncte.org
6	National Communications Association	natcom.org
7	National Women's Studies Association	nwsa.org
8	National Association for Ethnic Studies	ethnicstudies.org

There are many, many scholarly organizations and conferences. Please know that we have suggested just a few to get you started. Let's imagine you've found a conference you want to attend. Maybe you have lots of money and can easily travel to the conference. Since most of us don't have lots of money (wink), you may be able to apply for funding at your university to travel to the conference, or perhaps you can send a proposal to a conference that is being held near where you live.

The websites of scholarly organizations will have a Call for Proposals statement for their meeting. Read it. The Call for Proposals will help you think about the themes the organization is interested in. Is there a fit? Keep looking until the answer is "yes". Most academic associations will have a tab on the website where they explain how to submit a proposal. Sometimes they have very specific instructions. Don't be intimidated by those—they are meant to help you. Other times, there are no instructions about the content of the proposal. It really depends. Most websites will want your proposal to be a certain number of words (150–250, perhaps), and they will want you to select keywords that describe your work. They may also ask you to select an interest group or a sub-specialization of the larger group. Look for the one that is the best fit. They may also want you to pay for the conference when you submit your proposal, which isn't very nice. However, there is often a way to get a waiver for your conference registration, so that you can wait to pay until your paper is accepted. Scholarly organizations are non-profits and often run big conferences on precarious budgets. That's why they ask you to pay up front.

●●●●●

Catchy Title Here

How do you write a proposal to present a paper at a scholarly conference? The title you select for your presentation is important. If people are intrigued by the title, they may come to hear you speak. The title is a condensation of the idea of the paper. It should explain what will be addressed (but not how, why, or what your findings were). In many social science fields, it's common for the title to include a key quote from a recognized scholar followed by three concepts that situate the topic. Here's an example: "'My Grain of Sand for Society': Neoliberal Freedom, Language Learning, and the Circulation of Ideologies of National Belonging". What comes before the colon is a representative quote from what is discussed in the study. What comes after the colon tells us about the topics—language and ideologies—as well as the theoretical framework adopted for your study.

● ● ● ● ●
Keywords Matter

The keywords you choose are also important. Your keywords are how the reviewers for your proposal are selected, so be sure that your review category is clear. Often, people come to scholarly conferences to hear papers on particular subjects. Sometimes they select the sessions they attend based, in part, on the keywords you select. Imagine your paper were posted on the internet. What words would someone search to find it? Think of 5 to 10 words that you might use. Those are your keywords.

● ● ● ● ●
Getting Your Proposal Accepted

The proposal for presenting a conference paper is like an abstract for a scholarly paper. Think of it like an advertisement for your paper. Is it interesting? Is it well written? Does it explain what the question or theme is and how it is answered or addressed? Does it fit the word limit? If you use citations, don't include the reference list in the proposal. What follows are two examples of proposals for the American Anthropology Association. Both were accepted in different years, although they are quite different in form. Let's analyze them.

ULLMAN, CHAR Hiding in Plain Sight: Unauthorized Mexican Migrants, Language Use, and the Production of Public/Private Space

This paper, which is part of a larger, two-year ethnography, examines the linguistic/semiotic strategies that Rosenda (pseudonym), an unauthorized Mexican transmigrant, used to construct herself in the hotly contested classrooms and communities of Arizona. I discuss the ways Rosenda used Spanish, English, and translanguaging to create identity spaces in White Public Space, in her private sphere, and in the spaces in-between. Having migrated to the U.S. at the age of twelve to escape family violence, and seeing her job as a domestic worker as "something other than employment" (Hondagneu-Sotelo, 2001:9), an in-between space, Rosenda used linguistic/semiotic performances to challenge people who positioned her as undocumented. Using public pronouncements, workplace debates, and classroom discussions in her adult English classes, she strategically enacted outlaw discourses that transformed her social spaces into safe spaces for herself and others. I argue that escaping family violence is an understudied motive for migration (Parsons, 2010; Wagner, 2009), and that it profoundly impacts the agentive ways Rosenda inhabited social spaces through language use.

> **Working Together**
>
> What do you notice about the title? Is it good? Bad? Just OK? What was the context? What kind of methodology was used? What was the theoretical framework? What were the references? What were the findings?

Here is another one to consider:

ULLMAN, CHAR The Commodification of Language Learning and the Circulation of Ideologies of National Belonging

Inglés sin Barreras [English without Barriers] is an English-language program that is the progenitor of all self-study programs for Spanish speakers in the United States. It is also a pop-culture phenomenon. Retailing for up to $3,000 (with most people buying it at 21 percent interest), and comprised of books, DVDs, and CDs, *Inglés Sin Barreras* is the most advertised product on Spanish-language TV. More advertised in fact than Coca-Cola or McDonald's, ads for the program appear every 15 minutes from dawn to dusk on both Univisión and Telemundo. Jokes are made about it on *Sabado Gigante*, the popular television variety show; it is referred to in Spanish rap songs, and it was featured in the film *Spanglish*. For immigrants whose bodies, cultural practices, and languages are marginalized, migration is a "life-long process of negotiating identity, difference, and the right to fully exist in the new context" (Benmayor and Skotnes, 1994, p. 8). This paper discusses the ways in which ideologies of *Latindad* and national belonging to the United States for Latinos are circulated through *Inglés Sin Barreras*, the commodity. The author uses textual analysis of the program, along with interview data from Mexican migrants who have bought the program, to explore this theme.

> **Working Together**
>
> What do you think of this proposal's title? How is this proposal different from the previous one? How are references used? What is the theoretical framework? What kind of methodology was used? What are the findings?
>
> Sometimes the timing of when the proposals are due doesn't correspond well with your research process, and you have to send a proposal in before you really know what you've found. Can you guess which one of these proposals fits that category?

● ● ● ● ●

Presenting a Paper at a Conference

Many times, your presentation will be part of a panel of papers that share a theme in common. Usually you have 15–20 minutes to give your presentation. Find out from your professors or the conference organizers what the discourse norms are for the conference. Sometimes you're expected to talk to the audience and have PowerPoint slides to accompany the talk. Other times, you're expected to read your paper. It depends on the conference. For example, at the annual conference of the American Anthropological Association, each presenter usually gets 15 minutes to speak, and people read their papers at most sessions. Usually the chair of the session lets you know when you have five minutes left, three minutes, one minute, and then they tell you it's time to stop. This is usually done with slips of paper that have the times on them, a smart phone, or nonverbally with fingers raised in the air. If you speak at a medium pace, you can read a six-page paper that is double-spaced, with one-inch margins, in 12-point type, and finish in 15 minutes. But be sure to practice your presentation ahead of time. You should be a good citizen and not go over your allotted time. If you do, it means that someone else will get less time to speak because of you.

People who are attending your session are likely to ask questions of you and the other people on your panel. Remember, you only had 15 minutes or so to talk, and what you said may have sparked questions in their minds. Sometimes the questions they pose will lead you to think differently about your project. Maybe there is something you missed, or something you could analyze more appropriately with another approach. Don't worry. That's exactly what conferences are for. They help you learn how to think more deeply about your work. Some conferences have **discussants**. Discussants are usually senior scholars who (ideally) get copies of all the papers on a panel before the conference, and they write a paper that critiques the papers presented. They usually present their papers after everyone else has spoken. This can be scary. Sometimes people get humiliated by discussants. Other times they are congratulated on their brilliant work. Most of the time, it's something in between. Be open to what you might learn from what a discussant says. It's a great opportunity, even if you're scared.

Use your time at a scholarly conference to attend other presentations and meet recognized and other emerging scholars. Academics are usually excited to talk about their work and to engage with people who are interested in what they do. Don't hide in your room, read your paper, and leave. Conferences are times to learn and to discuss ideas. It's a valuable experience. Don't let fear keep you from learning and becoming part of the scholarly community.

●●●●●

Selecting a Scholarly Journal

Let's imagine that you got some good feedback about your paper at a conference. Maybe it came from your listening to different papers that started you thinking in a new way. Maybe it came from a conversation you had with someone. Or maybe it was something your discussant said. Now you have some ideas about how to approach your analysis differently. You're getting ready to turn your brief conference paper into a longer 35-page manuscript and submit it to a journal.

How do you get started? Your first step is to look at journals in the fields, to get a sense of the kinds of things they publish. Go to their websites and read the "Aims and Scope" for the journals. Do they line up with what you are doing in your piece? We like to "hang around" in certain journals to get a feeling for them. Here are some examples of journals that publish studies using the ethnography of communication approach:

Journals Char Likes	Journals Judy Likes
Anthropology & Education Quarterly	Language in Society
International Journal of Qualitative Research in Education	Journal of Linguistic Anthropology
Discourse: The Cultural Politics of Education	Discourse Processes
Linguistics and Education	International Journal of Business Anthropology
Race, Ethnicity and Education	Social Science and Medicine

The first thing you have to consider is whether or not you want to submit your manuscript to a refereed journal, the journal of a professional organization, a conference proceedings, an open-access journal, or a peer-reviewed journal. Let's go over the differences.

Refereed Journal

This one is tricky. Calling a journal refereed might be another way of saying it's peer-reviewed. Then again, it might not. Sometimes a refereed journal is one where a single editor determines all the journal content. Other times, it is the editor and the editorial board who decide what goes in the journal. If the editorial board includes a long list of well-known scholars, that's usually good, and it means that you're probably looking at a peer-reviewed journal. But sometimes the members of the editorial board aren't mentioned. If the editorial board isn't mentioned, it may be that the editor is the only one who referees the manuscripts. If the journal you're interested in says it's refereed and the website doesn't explain the peer-review process, then it may be fairly easy to get your work published there. But it may not be a very well-respected journal.

Journal of a Professional Organization

Most professional organizations have scholarly journals. The National Association of Bilingual Educators or the American Speech and Hearing Association are good examples. They publish articles that help practitioners, and while they are usually peer-reviewed, they often have higher acceptance rates, which means that they aren't as difficult to get into. There are also work-related journals, such as the *British Journal of Healthcare Assistants*, that publish opinion pieces and articles that focus on practical topics. Work-related journals may not be peer-reviewed—it really depends. The upside of these kinds of journals is that they often have wide readerships.

Conference Proceedings

Sometimes when you present your paper at a conference, the organization that sponsored the conference publishes conference proceedings. Publishing in conference proceedings can be a good way to break into scholarly publishing, as they are often peer-reviewed. Sometimes conference proceedings are published as a book; other times they are published like a journal. Sometimes scholarly organizations plan to publish proceedings, but they aren't able to follow through to publication, either because the people involved don't have time to work on it or because they don't have the money to complete the project. That's an issue that you can't control. The same thing can happen with scholarly journals, but it's not as common. Another concern about conference proceedings is that they can be difficult to find in a library's collection. But that shouldn't stop you, especially if this is your first foray into scholarly publishing.

Open-Access Journals

Open-access journals are a fairly new development in the world of academic publishing. In theory, they are a great idea. They make academic knowledge free and available to anyone who has internet access and is interested in a particular topic. The good news is that open-access journals can move from a manuscript to a published product very quickly, because they are exclusively online. Some open-access journals can publish a piece in one month. Traditional academic publishing can sometimes take years.

However, the most rigorous and well-respected journals in the social sciences typically aren't open-access ones, at least not yet. The top-tier journals are still those you need a university library card to access, or you pay for access to each article. When you buy access to an article, it costs about $30 per article. That can really add up.

There are different kinds of open-access journals, though. Some are sponsored by universities, scholarly organizations, or government agencies. For example, Michigan Publishing publishes open-access scholarly journals and is funded by the University of Michigan Libraries. You might want to peruse its holdings at http://www.publishing.umich.edu/publications/#journals.

There are also for-profit open-access journals, and they are . . . well, problematic. Typically, they charge what they call an "article processing fee", which can be from $100 to $2,000, to publish your article online. You read that correctly. But they may not tell you about the fee until your manuscript is almost ready for publication. Are you scratching your head, wondering why people would *pay* to have their articles published? Well, you're right. It doesn't make sense.

For people who are new to scholarly publishing (and we're thinking that might be you), it's important for you to learn about what are called "predatory publishers". These are publishers who look as though they have real academic journal websites, but, in fact, they are money-making ventures and they don't have a real peer-review process. They are trying to make money from people who don't have experience with scholarly publishing yet. Jeffrey Beall, a librarian at the University of Colorado Denver, publishes a terrific blog in which he keeps an exhaustive and well-maintained list of predatory academic publishers. You can read his blog at http://scholarlyoa.com. He has very explicit criteria as to what he thinks makes a journal predatory, and he publishes reviews of many publishers. It's a great idea to research the journal you're interested in and see if it's on Jeffrey's list before you decide to send off a manuscript.

Peer-Reviewed Journal

Peer-reviewed journals are the most prestigious scholarly journals. Peer-reviewed means that usually at least three scholars who share your specialization, along with the journal editor, will read and comment on your paper. The journal editor will let you know the direction he or she would like you to follow, as you may get conflicting advice from your reviewers. Peer reviewers are professors, usually very busy ones, and they write reviews as a professional courtesy. Sometimes they are slow in finishing their reviews. It's OK to contact the journal editor and ask how things are going. But remember, reviewers don't get paid for their work, and they take this aspect of the professoriate very seriously. It's not uncommon for a manuscript to take a year to get through the peer-review process. Of course, it can take less time, but it can also take more time.

There are different things to consider when you submit your manuscript to a peer-reviewed journal. First, you should think about the right fit. Is this the kind of journal that would publish a study like the one you've done? That's a really important point. The second thing to consider is that different journals have different **acceptance rates**. Sometimes it can be difficult to find out what those rates are. If you're a beginning scholar and this is the first paper you're submitting, it might be best to try for a journal that is more likely to accept your paper and then work your way up. We like to divide journals into three tiers:

Levels	Acceptance Rates
Tier 1	1%–20%
Tier 2	21%–49%
Tier 3	50% and up

There are three ways to find out about the acceptance rate of a journal. First, you can go to the journal's website to see if the acceptance rate is posted there. Sometimes it is. Another way to find out about acceptance rates is to use university databases that your library is likely to have. One database is called Cabell's International, and the other is called Ulrich's Periodicals. You can look for the journals you're interested in there and find out what the acceptance rates are. But those techniques don't always work. Sometimes the journal is listed, but there is no acceptance rate posted. Then, you have to try the last resort, which is to contact the editor of the journal by email. Because journals often have special issues, and that lessens the number of possible publication slots for everyone else, their acceptance rates can change significantly from year to year.

You may also see the **impact factor** on a journal's website or in a database. Impact factors are calculated each year, and they are based on how many scholars cite articles from those journals. It's a way of trying to understand how important a journal is, but, of course, it's an inexact science. However, you might consider the impact factor as one of the aspects of this decision-making process. Another thing to think about is the **Journal Citation Reports Ranking**. This is a more qualitative approach to understanding a journal's impact. However, not all journals are ranked through this system.

Finally, consider how frequently the journal publishes. If it publishes only once or twice a year, there aren't many slots for articles, compared to those journals that publish four or even six times a year.

There are a lot of things to consider as you get ready to share your knowledge.

●●●●●

Submitting a Manuscript

So let's imagine you've narrowed it down to three journals that might be good homes for your work. You have to figure out which one meets most of your criteria. Is the acceptance rate most important to you? The impact factor? Or perhaps you are interested in a journal that has a large readership. There are many things to think about. Once you've decided on that one journal, recognize that if the journal decides to review your manuscript, they are investing time and energy in your work, and they assume that you have submitted your manuscript to them in good faith, and to them and only them. Usually, when you do an electronic submission of the article, you have to check a box that says you haven't submitted it anywhere else, just to confirm that fact for the editor. You cannot send the same manuscript to multiple journals at the same time. It's bad form.

Next, you should look at the journal's website, and look at the section that is called something like "Author Guidelines" or "Instructions for Authors". That's where you will find out what publication style you should use. In the social sciences, American Psychological Association (APA) style is common. But you never know. The journal you think would be a good home might use the style guide of the Modern Language Association (MLA) or perhaps the University of Chicago (U of C). Be sure to find out which style you should use early in your process, so you only have to format things once. Sometimes journals have their own style guides. If that's the case, you need to follow that guide and get support from previous issues of the journal to find answers to questions you have that might not be dealt with on their style sheet.

We recommend that you send your manuscript to two to three friends, professors, or people in your field who have publishing experience. Tell them what journal you intend to submit your manuscript to and kindly ask them to review your work before you submit it. Once you've read their feedback, implement the suggestions that you think are the most useful. Make sure to remove all information that points to your identity from your manuscript. Save a copy that doesn't have your name on it, and in which any references to you in the paper itself or in the reference list are X'ed out. Now you are ready to submit this manuscript to a scholarly journal. We know it's been a long process to this point. And it's not over yet.

● ● ● ● ●

The Outcome

At this point, you might imagine that your manuscript is perfect, that it will fly through the review process, and that the reviewers will tell you they were honored to have read such brilliant work. While that's possible, it's more likely that your manuscript will fall into one of these three categories:

- Reject
- Revise and resubmit
- Accept with minor changes

There are two ways for a journal to **reject** your manuscript. The first is after the editor's review. The editor might look at your manuscript and decide it's not the right fit for the aims and scope of that journal. The editor might also decide that the writing or analysis is not good enough. If your manuscript is rejected this way, you will find out about it fairly quickly. What do you do? You look harder for the right journal, and/or you work on your writing or hire an editor.

The second way your manuscript could be rejected is by the peer reviewers. Journal editors hope that they catch manuscripts that are likely to be rejected before they send them out to reviewers, but sometimes things don't work out that way. It's possible that all three peer reviewers will reject your manuscript. Even if two of them make a strong case for rejecting it, and the editor is convinced, it can be rejected. That just means you rethink the relationship between your work and the journal. Perhaps you need to read and think more. Maybe you even need to collect more data, if that's possible. But it doesn't mean you should give up.

The most common response people get from the peer-review process is "**revise and resubmit**". It's so common that you might hear your professors say, "Sorry I can't go to your party. I have an R&R to do this weekend." For established scholars as well as emerging scholars, R&R isn't rest and relaxation—it's revise and resubmit.

When you get a revise and resubmit response from a journal, it's usually a very good thing. Almost every article that is ultimately published has gone through this process. So you're on your way! You will get a letter from the editor that attempts to synthesize and/or provide direction for you as you revise your work based on the attached reviews. You see, it's common for reviewers to ask you to do wildly different things. One may tell you to cut out a section, and the other may tell you to expand it. Another may praise your use of a particular scholar's work, and the other may condemn you for it. It's the editor's job to help you navigate these waters, by suggesting that you pay special attention to one of the reviewers over the others. That doesn't mean you should ignore what the others say; rather, when it comes to conflictive topics, the editor is suggesting a path that will help you to get your work published. At the same time, it's possible to disagree with a reviewer's suggestion. If you have a solid argument, the editor might just agree with you. When you submit your revisions to the journal's website, you will include a letter that details what each reviewer asked you to do and how you responded. If you didn't do something the reviewers asked for, you need to explain why.

Another outcome of the peer-review process might be that the reviewers accepted your manuscript virtually as is (with some minor changes that are mentioned in the letter from the editor), and you're basically ready for publication. That can happen. You never know.

Sometimes, researchers get discouraged by the amount of time and work involved in scholarly publishing. Please don't give up. Remember, you have the opportunity to share your knowledge and to contribute to what we as humans know. That's a significant contribution. You've already done a lot of work at this point in your project. Why not go the extra step and share your findings with a scholarly community? We encourage you to submit your manuscript for publication. We look forward to reading your work!

● ● ● ● ●

Summing Up *Methods for the Ethnography of Communication: Language in Use in Schools and Communities*

We hope this book has helped you learn to do the ethnography of communication. We realized that while there are a lot of textbooks that discuss this approach and related approaches, none takes you through the process, step-by-step. Until now. Judy and Char wanted a textbook like this to use in their own classes. We hope it has started you on the road to research, G-d willing.

This article and others that appear in various chapters as examples of ethnographic inquiry can be accessed through your university library, and the information you need to search for them is available in the References section at the end of this chapter:

● ● ● ● ●

References

Benmayor, R., & Skotnes, A. (1994). Migration and identity. New York: Oxford University Press.

Brooks, J.L. (2004). *Spanglish* [Motion Picture]. United States: Columbia Pictures.

Hondageu-Sotelo, P. (2001). *Doméstica: Immigrant Workers Cleaning and Caring the Shadows of Affluence*. Berkeley: University of California Press.

Parsons, N. (2010). "I Am Not [Just] a Rabbit Who Has a Bunch of Children!": Agency in the Midst of Suffering at the Intersections of Global Inequalities, Gendered Violence, and Migration, *Violence Against Women* 16: 881–901.

Wagner, H. (2009). Migration and Violence Against Women—Very Invisible: Basic Migration and Re-negotiation of the Migration Process, *Anthropos* 104: 41–61.

Index ●●●●●

acceptance rates 177
Agar, Michael 65, 66
agency 119
American Anthropological
    Association 173
analysis 46, 50, 54
Anzaldua, Gloria 34
Appaduri, Arjun 35
Arab/Arabic 67, 73, 74
artifact collection 41, 46, 51, 53, 54,
    76, 82, 87, 89
Athey, Chris 52
Axiom 1: Data Never Speaks for Itself
    32
Axiom 2: Doing Social Research Is a
    Rhetorical Activity 33

Bachman, Lyle 13
Bakhtin, Mikhail 35, 67
Barlett, F. C. 63
Bhabba, Homi K. 35
bias 4, 52, 65, 68
bilingual/bilingualism 122, 123, 124,
    125, 126, 127, 128, 129, 130, 131,
    132, 133, 134, 135, 136, 137, 138,
    139, 140, 141, 142, 143
binaries 1, 46, 77
borders/borderlands 34, 72, 82, 83
Bourdieu, Pierre 35, 47, 72
Bowles, S., and H. Gintis 32
Butler, Judith 35

Calavera Catrina 89
Canale, Michael, and Merrill Swain 12
Carlson, Julie 154
Chicana 34, 35
Chitling Test of Intelligence (Dove)
    68
Chomsky, Noam 15, 16
Christianity/Christian 66, 67
Christian Pentecostal Assembly of
    God 66, 67, 68
citizenship 161, 162
class 48
classroom environment 5, 51, 52, 65,
    66, 68, 69

Cliffords, James, and George Marcus
    20
collaborative ethnography 152
Collaborative Institutional Training
    Initiative (CITI) 56
communication 19, 55, 67, 71, 96,
    106
communicative competence 12, 13,
    16, 49, 65, 66, 68, 70
community 5, 7, 8, 9, 11, 40, 42, 43,
    44, 45, 50, 52, 53, 54, 55, 65, 66,
    68, 69, 70, 73, 83, 84, 85, 87, 88,
    90, 102, 114, 120, 122, 132, 133,
    151, 166, 168
community of practice 16, 20, 23, 44,
    45, 52, 53, 70, 77, 87, 114, 122,
    149, 155, 157
competent/competence 10, 11, 12,
    13, 15
compile your knowledge 52, 60
conference 169, 170, 171, 173, 175
consciousness 3
consent forms 58
consumer research 80
content analysis 94
Convertino, Christina 105, 106, 113,
    134
cultural groups 4
cultural interpretations 4
cultural knowledge 3, 4, 9, 68, 69
culture/s 2, 3, 4, 49, 66, 67, 68, 73, 77
culture, characteristics of 3,4
CULTURES Model 46, 49, 50, 51, 132,
    149, 152, 154, 160, 167
curander@ 24

data: checking of 150; collection of
    46, 50, 53, 54, 55, 62
Davies, B. 42
D'Costa, Krystal 120, 121
deductive inquiry 39
discourse competence 13, 155
discursive practices 42
discussants 173
document collection 54
Dressman, Mark 29, 32, 33

language socialization 121, 122, 123, 124, 125, 126, 127, 128
langue 15, 16
Lassiter, Luke E. 42
Lather, Patti 50
Latindad 172
Laundra, Kenneth, and Tracy Sutton 68
Lave, Jean, and Etienne Wenger 16, 45, 70
leading question/s 85
learning 11, 51, 65, 66, 67
LeCompte, Margaret D. and Jean J. Schensul 156
Lefebure, Henri 36
lesbian/lesbianism 8
Lesbian Separatism 8
LGBTQ 9
Lichtman, Marilyn 162
Lincoln, Yvonne S. and Egon G. Guba 150
linguistic anthropology and sociolinguistics 15
locate patterns/patterns 51, 53, 60, 62, 72, 73, 74, 93, 94, 101, 102, 105, 118, 159, 165
looking at practices and norms 70, 71

MacNamara, Patricia 50
macro-level analysis 94, 96, 114, 129, 130, 160, 164
Marx, Karl 32, 62, 71
material culture 89
McCurdy, David, James Spradley, and Diana Shandy 84, 85
member checks 54, 149, 150, 151, 152, 153, 154, 155, 157
memory 11
mestizaje 34
Mexico/Mexican 6, 84, 85, 86, 114, 115, 121, 122, 171
micro-level analysis 94, 96, 103, 114, 129, 130, 160, 163, 164
mid-level analysis 94, 96, 100, 105, 114, 129, 130, 160, 164
migration 71, 82
Milgram, Stanley 57
Mills, C. Wright 7
mini-tour questions 84
morphology 17
Mortimer, Katherine 122, 123, 124, 125, 126, 127, 128, 130, 133, 134, 138, 139

multiple modalities 16, 70, 72, 98
Muslim/s 86, 87

Naaeke, Anthony, et al 22
Native American youth 71
'native' ethnographer/s 43
Navajo 71
Nazism 56
neoliberal 116, 117
new-instrument theory 31, 32
norms 10, 11, 103, 119, 120, 121, 129
NVivo 162

observation 76, 79, 81
observer's paradox 39
open-access journals 175
outcome, the 179
overlapping speech 98

Pappas, C. C., and E. Tucker-Raymond 77
Paraguay 122, 123, 124, 125, 126, 127, 128, 129, 130, 131, 132, 133, 134, 135, 136, 137, 138, 139, 140, 141, 142, 143, 145
parenting 115, 116, 117
parole 15, 16, 17
participant observation 39, 40, 41, 42, 46, 52, 53, 54, 77, 80, 82, 106, 107, 108, 109, 110, 111, 112, 113, 114, 115, 145, 151, 155, 160
performance 15
periphery 44, 53, 70, 71, 84, 119
phonemic/phonetic 23
phonology 17
Piaget, Jen 52
Pike, Kenneth 23, 24
pitch 98
playback 155
pollero/coyote 85
position/positionality 4, 21, 46, 47, 48, 60, 61
positivism 24, 30, 39
postmodern/postmodernism/ postmodern turn 19, 44
postponing judgment 46, 48
power relations 68
practice/practice theory 72, 73, 74, 80, 81
pragmatics 18
praxis 42
primary discourse 13
prior knowledge 7, 52